FISHING FOR FISH
NOT IN THE POND

(52 Essays)

FISHING FOR FISH NOT IN THE POND

[FIFTY-TWO ESSAYS]

By

DR. ROBERT W. McLAUGHLIN

Essay Index Reprint Series

BOOKS FOR LIBRARIES PRESS

FREEPORT, NEW YORK

First Published 1930
Reprinted 1968

LIBRARY OF CONGRESS CATALOG CARD NUMBER:

68-20315

PRINTED IN THE UNITED STATES OF AMERICA

Introduction

The rich and lasting values of these essays by Dr. Robert W. McLaughlin is easily predictable by those who know him. This has been my privilege for nearly thirty years past: years filled with an increasing admiration for his gifts and scholarship and a growing affection for him as a servant of God and the people.

He captured my mind years ago with his able book, "The Relation of Washington and Lincoln in the Federal Constitution." Later came his beautiful character sketch, "Caleb Matthews," which has gone through many editions. Two years ago his masterly philosophical work, "The Spiritual Element in History," appeared and satisfied my expectations, which in all conscience were high enough. Now comes this volume of sane, strikingly original essays with the suggestive title, "Fishing for Fish Not in the Pond."

What interests me in this volume is the skill with which Dr. McLaughlin uses his method. Each essay deals with a single vital truth of life; also, somewhere in each essay this truth is connected with a statement in the Bible. That a truth about life should be supported by a quotation from scripture is not strange. For the Bible is the great storehouse of wisdom and guidance. Its literary beauty enshrines these treasures in the amber of a perfect style. Its moral supremacy safeguards the dearest interests we have.

But Dr. McLaughlin goes farther than this. Most writers who have to maintain a steady output observe life and then write about what they observe. In doing so, they think that they retain the human element in their work. The defect with this method is that the mind is so constructed that it sees what it wants to see. The result is these essayists soon find themselves moving within a narrow range of interests. Not so with Dr. McLaughlin. He goes to the Bible with its prose, poetry, histories, prophesies, parables, proverbs, and biographies for his thoughts, and then applies these to life as observed and experienced. The result is his essays move within a vast range of interests. Evidence of this is found in the titles of these essays. For these titles are in themselves sermons or addresses for thoughtful business and professional people.

Nevertheless, until recently journalism has been chary of any mention of the Bible in its columns. Doubtless there have been sufficient reasons for this reluctance. Too many would-be expositors simply record their own impressions of the Bible. When we look beneath their rhetorical draperies for the vitality of the Book itself, it is not there. They have taken away its strength, breadth, and saliency, and we know not where they have laid them.

Happily Dr. McLaughlin has long since learned the art of undertaking spiritual and intellectual adventures in a perfectly human way. His pungent, often humorous, and frequently luminous characterizations in these essays enlist the attention of the average man. There is nothing formal or stilted in his manner of approach. Our thoughts are concentrated upon pivotal truths keenly and sometimes brilliantly applied to actual living.

I cannot close this insufficient tribute without saying that he has fulfilled an extraordinary task in an extraordinary way. There is nothing trite or banal in these pages. They pulsate with life and its sagacious interpretations. That brevity which is the soul of art and sound judgment is stamped upon them. Here is another and a splendid example of the author's ability to bring forth truths ever old but ever new from the noblest literature extant.   S. Parkes Cadman.

Radio Minister of the Federal
Council of Churches in America.

Table of Contents

Table of Contents

Fishing for Fish Not in the Pond

A GLIMPSE of Andrew Carnegie on a summer day years ago remains vividly in my memory. Out from Stockbridge, in the Berkshire hills, he was seen seated in a row boat on the pond near the road. With mental health shattered, the steel king spent hours each pleasant day fishing in the pond for fish that were not there. He did this, because he thought himself on the beautiful and well-stocked lake of his magnificent estate in Scotland.

The scene was a pathetic one. This once masterful man futilely holding a fish pole. But if the sight touched my heart, it also started my mind working. As the imposing mansion, beautiful grounds, and the aged millionaire steel king in his little boat were left behind, the question arose in my mind, How rich are you? So, taking a hasty inventory of my life as the motor car rolled along the roadway, this is what I found.

First, a reasonably clear mind in a sound body, having enough of a mind to know when to come in out of the rain, and a robust body, my wealth conservatively estimated would be in seven figures. For the shattered man in the boat, had he the power of choice, would gladly have given me millions of his wealth for a return of his health.

Second, a gift of appreciation. On this lovely

1

summer morning I enjoyed the singing of birds, breathed in the balmy air, feasted my eyes on the encircling hills, and smiled at children in the roadway. Just to react with appreciation to the wonders of God's world, and be thankful that you are alive, is worth not a penny less than a million.

Third, the inventory showed some convictions. In the vicissitudes of life certain truths had reached down below the level of opinions and had become convictions worth being loyal to and living with. Here by any fair appraisal is another million.

Fourth, some friendships are found in the inventory. The one who has been a companion and the mother of my children—at least a million. Children each of them worth not less than a million. A few comrades who have wintered and summered with me, and stood by me when I needed help—upwards of half a million apiece.

Fifth, the fact of being alive and ready to move forward and accept responsibility and opportunity. In the business world today much is made of the value of being a going concern. Why not in life? The once canny little Scotsman in the boat was no longer a going concern. But, in the goodness of God, some of my days were ahead. If so, the chance to toil, to serve and to love is worth a good round million.

But I must stop or the income man will be after me. For I have made myself out on a conservative basis a multi-millionaire. And such any man is who has a normal mind in a sound body, a gift of appreciation, a few convictions, some genuine friends and a fair chance to live his life. For in the words of the Psalmist, "More to be desired are they than gold, yea, than much fine gold."

So, my heart was filled with pity for the once masterful Andrew Carnegie, now sleeping at night in one of the more than hundred rooms of his huge mansion, and in the daytime fishing for fish not in the pond. He seemed desperately poor; I, tremendously rich.

Genius Goes Visiting

I BELIEVE that the bow-legged, near-sighted, bald-headed, big-nosed, short-of-stature little Hebrew named Paul is the greatest imperfect human whose name flashes from the page of history.

He was a genius of the spiritual, not a mere restless wanderer on the higher levels. Write a tragedy, compose a symphony, paint a picture, chisel a block of marble, establish a new method in research, or make a fundamental invention. But to walk steadily along the lofty stretches of the spiritual requires a higher order of genius.

Being a genius he made a memorable visit to another man. "I went up to Jerusalem to visit Peter, and tarried with him for fifteen days," so the Bible says. The question is, Why did this remarkable man set apart fifteen days for a visit with a particular man named Peter who lived at the time in the city of Jerusalem?

The question becomes interesting when it is remembered that these two men represented different types. Rousseau thought he was saying something striking when he wrote, "I am unlike anyone I have even seen." But he was mistaken. Every human being is unlike every other human being. Individuality reaches down to the molecules of the blood. There are, however, contrasted types of character. Paul differed from Peter as John Marshall differed from Thomas

Jefferson or Benjamin Disraeli differed from William E. Gladstone. He was of select stock, city bred, wealthy, university trained—an aristocrat; Peter was of humble origin, country bred, poor, unlettered—a democrat. Yet the aristocrat goes out of his way to visit a democrat!

Something wonderful came into the life of Peter because of a visit from Paul. Can you imagine having Shakespeare, Beethoven or Isaac Newton as a guest in your home for fifteen days? This was the never-to-be-forgotten experience of Peter. Under his roof and at his table for more than two weeks was a magistral person whose imperial intellect was probing deeply the meaning of life.

But if this visit meant much to Peter the democrat, it meant even more to Paul the aristocrat. Although a spiritual genius, or perhaps because he was a spiritual genius, he was in a questioning mood. For on the Damascus road a strange and shattering experience had come to him. Was it genuine? It came in the withering heat of the noon hour when he was tired and hungry. Was this experience a mere fiction of his overwrought imagination due to the fact that physically he was below par? In other words, had he evolved it out of his inner consciousness?

At Jerusalem is Peter. He had actually known Jesus. He must talk with this fisherman. So, to the big city he goes and seeks him out. Picture the two men together for 15 days—Paul asking and Peter answering questions about the mighty Galilean!

Here are the credentials of genius. Restless and eager in the search for truth. Ever visiting. Goethe died with a book in his hand. Michael Angelo died with his boots on, having worked during the day on his statue, "Pieta." Paul is no longer young. But he must know more about the central interest of his life. Hence the visit to Peter.

The man he seeks is out of his own class. But, being a genius, he knows no class. He will learn from anyone, anywhere, and at any time. With generations of culture in his blood and a university education in his head, he will humbly sit at the feet of a simple, stalwart, unlettered fisherman— for he is a genius who goes visiting that he may find truth.

Why Be So Serious?

"BE not righteous overmuch; neither make thyself overwise: why shouldest thou destroy thyself?" What will you do with these words? If you take them literally you are in trouble. For at their face value, these words seem to teach that it is possible to have too much of righteousness and too much of wisdom. Yet in actual life none of us has more of righteousness or wisdom than is good for him. Each of us in the development of his character can make use of an unlimited amount of goodness and insight.

To catch the thought of the ancient philosopher in this utterance, imagination and humor are needed. The words are to be accepted as suggestive rather than precise. From this angle the thought would seem to be something like this: In seeking to win character through the possession of righteousness and wisdom which are fundamental in strong character, avoid the danger of taking yourself too seriously—a common fault in life.

Let us hasten to add, that these words afford no justification for taking our relation to the world in which we live as other than serious business. Margaret Fuller, in a patronizing mood, remarked that she had decided to accept the universe. When her remark was repeated to Carlyle his comment was, "Gad, she'd better." So with all of us. Here is this big, realistic, mysterious, buzzing, thump-

7

ing something called the world. Not to take it seriously is to act like the animal with the long ears.

Also, a man can find in these words no warrant for taking his own life as anything less than serious. Many are trying to do this. A New York newspaper tells of the death of a young artist in Greenwich Village. He had been denied the recognition that he thought his ability entitled him to receive. So he decided to secure attention at the brief moment of his departure. With this in mind he wrote a note and then took the poison. After his death, on the table by his bed the following was found: "Life is a rare bit dream. Ha, ha! such a funny dream. But enough, I am ready to awake to something less ridiculous."

The poor fellow in trying to treat life flippantly became inartistic. He attempted to be facetious and was merely hectic. He thought to put up a brave front only to whistle while going through the graveyard. Experience demands that the world and each man's life in the world be taken seriously. Although learned in childhood the words are not outgrown, "Life is earnest, life is real."

Yet it is possible to take ourselves too seriously, and in doing so, bungle the business of taking the world and life seriously. That is, it is possible to allow the strength of a wholesome seriousness to degenerate into the weakness of an overstrained seriousness. What is meant is suggested by the singer who crowds the voice instead of letting the sound come out freely; by the pianist who thumps the keys instead of giving them the artist's touch;

by the young barbarian football player getting away before the whistle blows and so penalizing the team for offside play; by the golfer stepping up to the tee and pressing, only to send the ball into the tall timber, when he should follow through and see the ball sail away down the fairway.

So, the man who takes himself too seriously, crowds the voice, thumps the keys, gets away before the whistle blows, and slices the ball in the game of life. He needs to ponder the meaning of these words in the Bible, and accept them as a warning. For a good man should be at his best.

The Coöperative Thinker

WHEN you come upon a growing person you always find a coöperative thinker. His personality is expanding and he is becoming increasingly efficient, because he knows how to place his mind along side of other minds. This is what the philosopher in the Bible means when he says:

> "Where there is no counsel, purposes are
> disappointed,
> But in the multitude of counsellors they
> are established."

In order to have genuine coöperation there must be a mingling not a merging of minds. The merger idea is in the air and is being worked to the limit. It may be sound in business, although there is a suspicion that it is being pushed too far. But it has no value in thinking. In the field of thought the product of the merger idea is the "herd thinker," who is in our midst and whose number is legion. Through adroit manipulation by the few, the thoughts of the many are controlled. Here is at once the power and the peril of propaganda, which is simply advertising applied to thoughts instead of to things.

Seeking to be a coöperative thinker it is well to keep in mind that the end sought is truth. In the debates in legislative halls, there is something of mental coöperation as in the clash of minds glints

10

of truth flash forth. But the kingdom of God will never come through legislation, because the aim is party victory rather than truth. Likewise in the "lay your cards on the table" method employed in industrial disputes, there is considerable coöperation. Yet the aim sought is compromise, not truth. The genuine coöperative thinker who is expanding in personality is always looking beyond compromise or victory. He seeks to know the liberating power of truth.

To have real coöperation there must be a mingling of personalities on the basis of respect and sympathy. This involves breaking through the restrictions imposed upon us by the particular conditions of our lives. The poet Arthur H. Clough presented himself to Florence Nightingale, and asked for work. His restriction was the scholarly atmosphere of Oxford in which he had dwelt for years. He felt that he must break through, and in doing a bit of practical work gain a deeper insight into life.

Each of us needs to break through his individual restriction. If in robust health, call upon a sick person; if rich in worldly goods, know intimately a poor man; if of sedentary habits, have among your friends those who work with their hands; if of scholarly attainments, maintain contact with practical men; if of one religious faith, keep in touch with those of other faiths; if a native, seek those who are foreigners; and if a saint, be sure and cultivate those who are sinners—for even sinners can teach saints.

Elihu H. Root was a leading corporation lawyer of his day. He has made the statement that when he needed intellectual stimulus, he spent an evening at the meeting of a labor union. To do this, he had to break through the restriction imposed upon him by the fact that he was a corporation lawyer. Is it any wonder that recently this remarkable man, well beyond 80 years of age, crossed the ocean to represent his country at the delicate deliberations in connection with the World Court? He was chosen to serve his country because he is a coöperative thinker.

Foundation and Heavy Timbers

MAN is a political, religious, thinking and social animal. As such he has created for himself the state, school, church and family. These are the big four—the four institutional sides forming the foundation upon which society rests.

So runs the current thought regarding the composition of society. Yet, the thought is not altogether true. For in thinking in this way, the implication is that the church, school, state and family are of equal importance. A more accurate statement would be that society is the superstructure that rests upon the heavy timbers of the church, school and state, which in turn lean upon the family as the foundation.

Notice that almost at the beginning of the Bible narrative, and long before any other institution is mentioned, words about the family are found: "Therefore shall a man leave his father and his mother, and shall cleave to his wife."

The location of these words in the Bible suggests that the family is the oldest of human institutions. Man may be a political, religious and thinking animal. But he lived for centuries before he sought to express himself in the state, church and school. Further, during these centuries, he doubtless expressed crudely through his family life the functions which later he expressed in more

13

perfect form in the church, state and school. Moreover, the other institutions could come into existence only on the basis of family life.

Precisely this is true today. The state, school and church when they function properly have much to contribute to the family. But the family as it performs its mission has more to contribute to these institutions. They are dependent upon the family; the family can be independent of them. You cannot think of these institutions as existing without the family. But the family can be thought of as existing without these institutions.

An example will make this clear. Some miles off the coast, on a rock in the Atlantic is a lighthouse. Its inhabitants are the keeper, his wife, two children, the assistant keeper, his wife, and one child. Each Sunday under the guidance of the keeper and with the wife of the assistant at the organ, the group gathers for worship. Here is the church. On five mornings of the week the three little children assemble and are taught by the wife of the keeper, who before her marriage was a teacher. Here is the school. And these seven human beings, miles from the nearest settlement, are a society in themselves. Here is the state.

This illustration from actual life indicates that should the school cease to exist, some degree of education could be carried on in the home. Should the church go out of existence, there would remain family worship. Likewise, should the state disappear, families could be organized into miniature states.

The point is the family is fundamental. If today there is a lessening of respect for law in the state, a lowering of spiritual tone in the church, and a let down in character training in the school, the cause will be found in family life. For the family is the foundation, and these other institutions are the heavy timbers. And being heavy timbers they need a strong foundation.

The Supreme Masterpiece

IT was a gray day, with a soft drizzle of rain outside, so the picture light within, as the art critics would say, was correct. Under these conditions a quiet and thoughtful hour was spent in the Dresden Art Gallery, reacting to the beautiful Sistine Madonna of Raphael.

Although the subject is spiritual, the treatment by the artist, in the best sense of the word, is worldly. A couple of saints, to be sure, are on their knees in the attitude of worship, but their faces indicate curiosity rather than reverence. The mischief in the eyes of the cherubs, who come up into the picture from below, suggests that they could make things lively in any home. And the face of the Madonna, while surpassingly lovely, has no subtle imprint of the sacred experience, when, overshadowed by the Holy Spirit, she gave birth to the Saviour of the World.

This impression of the picture may seem strange to those who have never seen the original. Yet a beautiful, none too deep, and worldly interpretation is what you would expect from the gay, handsome and marvelously gifted Raphael, who could carve golden plates for banquets with the same faultless perfection that he could paint saints for churches.

Still, if unmoved spiritually by the two saints, the delightful little cherubs and the lovely Ma-

16

donna, the picture awed me into silence. Here was glorious art with the freshness of this morning's sunrise, although executed more than four hundred years ago. Here, like glints of lights seen through the trees of a forest, was genius shining through the technique of line and color. For one never-to-be-forgotten hour I gazed upon a masterpiece of the world!

Reacting to the genius of a master craftsman, there came to the surface of my mind the familiar story of his drawing a circle. He called, you remember, to see a friend. Finding him out, and about to go away, the servant asked his name. He took a card and drew a circle, which he handed to the servant as his reply. When the friend returned and was given the card by the servant, he knew who had called, for among his acquaintances Raphael alone could with free hand draw a perfect circle.

But what about the baby in the arms of the Madonna? This incident of the circle on the calling card caused me to fasten my gaze upon the baby. Then a miracle was performed, for miracles occur today as in olden days. The infant with its sweet little tousle head close to the face of its beautiful mother began to grow before my very eyes. He grew into a child playing in the fields, into a boy going to school, into a stalwart youth working at the carpenter's bench, into a young man moving through cities and villages preaching glad tidings and performing deeds of mercy, and finally into a holy one dying on a cross for a cause more dear to him than his own life.

Then an angel seemed to speak to me, for I also believe in angels. He uttered three words of the Bible about this innocent little babe in the picture who became the Holy One in history. The words were, "Yet without sin"—the most astounding and absolutely unique words ever uttered concerning a human being.

With these words ringing in my soul, as I left the Art Gallery the thought shaped itself something like this: Raphael with pigment on canvas, in painting the Sistine Madonna, drew the perfect circle of art. Christ, with laughter and tears, drew in terms of conduct the perfect circle of life. The artist wrought mightly and by creating a masterpiece is among the immortals. The Son of Man wrought still mightier and dwells forever in the white light that beats about the throne of God. Because of this, He is the supreme masterpiece.

Are You Superior or Mediocre?

SOME flowers in the field greet you like banners waving; other flowers have to be discovered in out of the way places. So with the truths of the Bible.

Working my way through a long, dreary, geneological chapter of names and numbers in the Bible my eye caught these words: "Men who had understanding of their times, to know what Israel ought to do." Coming upon these pregnant words unexpectedly was like finding a sturdy little flower peeping out from under a decayed log in a swamp or a delicate blue bell growing in the fissure of a rock by the ocean shore. Seeing them, these vibrant words said to me at once, "Here is superiority in the midst of mediocrity."

But have these words meaning today? Are there groups in America of whom it can be said, "They are superior in the sense that they understand the times in which we live and so know what the nation should do."

The times have changed. Historians tells us that we are living in the third age of civilization— the machine age. These men of the Old Testament lived in the agricultural age. How different our machine age from that far away agricultural age. Perhaps it was easier to understand the times in those early days, although as the result of im-

19

proved means of communication the world of our
day is much smaller.

Then we are told that the striking characteristic
of our machine age is the rapidity with which
changes are taking place, due to the restless on
march of science. And this is true. Still, if the
times change, the need of men who understand
the times remains unchanged. In fact, there was
never a moment in history when the demand was
so insistent for groups of people intelligent enough
to interpret the trend of events as the present moment.

Such groups of people are especially necessary
in a nation like ours, if the leadership of exceptional individuals is to prove effective. Contrary
to the doleful predictions made by European ob-
servers in the early years, the Republic has been
prolific in giving forth from its loins great men.
And there is no evidence that the Republic has exhausted its power. Our danger is not in our inability to produce outstanding leaders but in
expecting too much of these leaders and not enough
of intelligent groups of citizens in all parts of the
land.

For, let us remember that governmental leaders
are never prophets. They have no uncanny skill in
seeing around the corner. Abraham Lincoln is the
greatest leader of government our nation has pro-
duced. Yet he so lacked in prophetic insight that
he was compelled to shift his position on slavery
four times in six years. And his last position com-
pletely contradicted his first position.

No, the leader in whom the people have confidence is one who controlled by prudence and guided by expediency, moves forward under the pressure of an enlightened public opinion. This he can do, only as groups exist in the nation who possess a superiority in the midst of mediocrity.

The encouraging feature in the situation is that thousands of such groups are functioning in America at the present time. For example, visualize the Church as it is found in city, village, and at the crossroads. Every true church, of whatever name or creed, is or should be an aristocracy in the midst of a democracy of voters. In this sense the Church as an aristocracy must always be in politics. But let me hasten to add, it must be an aristocracy of intelligence and character.

The Nobodies of History

HISTORY is made by four classes of people. Those cast in imperial mould who achieve exceptionally and whose names stand forth—Julius Caesar, Dante, Shakespeare, and Lincoln. These are the somebodies of history. Another class is composed of those who possess some peculiarity and so reach the page of history. The strongest man—a Samson shattering the pillars of the temple; the most cruel man—a Nero fiddling while Rome burned; the richest man—a Croesus exhibiting his wealth to Solon; the longest lived man—a Methuselah breaking all records for longevity. These are the odd bodies of history. A third and much larger class is made up of those about whom something is known and whose names are recorded. They are found on church rolls, roster of regiments, and memorial tablets. Some cause or institution preserves their names and service rendered. These are the everybodies of history. Still a fourth class consists of those whose sheer existence only is known through the work they did. Their names are unknown. These are the nobodies of history—a name used with the utmost appreciation and the deepest reverence.

The nobodies are numerically the strongest. The everybodies whose names in small print have reached the page of history are indeed numerous. There are so many that the Bible speaks of them

as the "hundred and forty and four thousand."
But the Bible speaks of the nobodies as the "multitude that no man can number."

Using the metaphor of history a river, the nobodies are the growth in the stream that never reaches up from below, but whose existence is known by the dark patches of color on the surface. They speak to us from the past in massive pyramids by the Nile, in lofty cathedrals on the continents, in magnificent palaces at royal capitols, and in other great construction enterprises.   Like a vast cloud of witnesses they surround us at every turn in the present.   In the morning while sipping the coffee of the breakfast that is sweetened with sugar and diluted with cream they come thronging in from plantation, everglade, and farm.   Going forth for the day's work unnamed but actual they go with us in the pavement on which we tread, the vehicle in which we ride, and the building in which we toil. And when at night the eyes close in sleep they are near at hand in the bed on which the tired body rests and the blankets that cover the body.

When the pilgrim at Rome requested a relic, the Pope's reply was, "Go to the Coliseum and gather a handful of dust."   The words were not only profoundly true but prophetic of a new day. For modern historical scholarship through its emphasis upon economic forces, social institutions, and cultural influences is reminding us as never before of the mighty part played by the nobodies in the making of history.

This thought about the nobodies as the dominant

force in the creating of civilization takes on a sacred meaning as Armistice Day is observed. Reacting to the tendency in modern historical study, the most significant outcome of the World War has been the recognition by the governments of the unnamed heroes who toiled, suffered, and died. So, the symbolical tomb has been reared, and with solemn pomp and reverent pageantry has been dedicated to the memory of the unnamed nobodies —the Unknown Soldier.

But in heaven there are no unknown soldiers. If their names never reach the page of history on earth, they are caught up into heaven and written in the Book of Life. For God, who observes the fall of the tiny sparrow does not overlook those who gave themselves that others might live.

Why Are You Dull?

DULL people are found in unexpected places. A good person ought to be the last in the world to be dull. Yet it was said of a certain man that he was so dully good that he made even virtue disreputable. A big business man should never be dull. But Theodore Roosevelt, when President, said he dreaded meeting railroad presidents because they were so uninteresting. Those with large wealth and an abundance of leisure ought to be anything but dull. The facts, however, are otherwise.

Recently I traveled to Florida aboard one of the de luxe trains composed largely of drawing rooms and compartments. It was a positive relief at Jacksonville to change to a day coach in which were men in their shirt sleeves and women tending children. Why? Because on the de luxe train were overfed and underexercised men and women on their way down the East Coast to places where hotel managers chloroform guests and take away their money. For sheer yawning insipidity this rich crowd could not be beaten. To pass into the day coach and see families eating luncheons from boxes and to hear babies cry, was like going into another and better world.

But if dullness is met with where least expected, the absence of dullness is encountered in unlooked-for places. I know a dear little old lady, with wrinkles in her face and crow feet under her eyes, that for charming vivacity I will match against any scintillating débutante in America. Seated in her rocking chair by the window, on the sill of which are her potted plants, she is an antique, quaint, unique character such as you see in pictures, read about in story books, and once in a while have the good fortune to know in real life. An hour in her company is worth an evening at the best play in any theater in the city. Age has nothing to do with dullness.

In front of my house a gang of laborers have been at work for weeks. One of the laborers is a big husky fellow, with skin black as a lump of coal. He smiles at the children and they smile at him as they pass. At the noon hour while eating with a score of other laborers he is the center of the group. He has in his own way precisely what the aged woman has—charm. At a conservative estimate, the public utility company could afford to pay him double wages because of the enlivening influence he exerts upon the other workmen. Dullness is not a question of the kind of work you do.

What is the cause of dullness? One is the doing a thing, however important that may be, to the exclusion of other things. This is the trouble with railroad presidents. They may manage railroads that are double-tracked, but their minds run on single tracks.

Another cause is having too many things and expecting too much from the things. This is the trouble with rich people today. Jesus saw deeply into life when He said, "It is easier for a camel to pass through the eye of a needle than for a rich man to enter the kingdom of heaven." The average rich person with an abundance of leisure would be out of place in heaven. For in heaven only interesting people will feel at home.

The Sardonic Playfulness
of Fame

"NOW a new king arose in Egypt who knew not Joseph." Do not feel sorry for Joseph but be ashamed of the king. You remember the dinner party in London at which Thomas Carlyle was present. As most of those present were artists the conversation was about the merits of a canvas by Titian. Not being interested in art, and having remained quiet for sometime, finally Carlyle blurted out, "Who is Titian? That is another fact about him." "No," replied one of the guests at the table, "that is a fact about Carlyle." And the laugh was on the dour Scotsman. So with the new king in Egypt. Like Carlyle and his ignorance of Titian, this king boasted that he knew not the great man by name, Joseph. And while he boasted fame laughed at him over its shoulder. For the king, unnamed, lives on the page of history because of his ignorance.

Fame not only laughs at those who should know, it indulges in pranks at the expense of those who should be known. For, strange as it seems, it will perpetuate a man's achievement and ignore the man himself. Its sardonic playfulness is like the cat playing with the mouse it would kill.

Someone made a compass. The era of exploration in the 15th and 16th centuries was made possible because of this compass. Another hit upon the

idea of building a chimney, and changed houses
from hovels, into which human beings crawled to
find protection from the elements, to livable
homes. Still another used sand in such a way as to
produce transparent glass, making feasible windows
through which the light and warmth could pass.
These are epochal inventions. Yet the names of
those who wrought mightily are utterly unknown.
Fame has played a cruel prank.

The playfulness of fame is sometimes impish
rather than cruel. It consists in attaching names
to things while causing the personalities back of
the names to fade out.

At the lunch counter you ordered a sandwich,
never thinking that the two slices of bread with
meat (not much) between, takes its name from an
Earl in England. You enjoyed an overnight ride
in a sleeper, and cared nothing about the story of
the cabinet maker named Pullman, who made possible the comfortable journey. You spent an evening with your radio, unmindful of the fact that
almost every part of the contrivance has the name
of an inventor of whom you probably know nothing—Watt, Ampere, Volta, and others.

So, a worthwhile achievement is no assurance of
fame; likewise, a name perpetuated. Fame to be
real must visualize a personality along with an
achievement connected with a name. Give the
money to build the library or endow the college,
with the condition that it take your name. But
while the money is being given fame will be laughing at you. For like the snowflake falling into the

stream, with the passing of the years your personality will melt away.

Fame deals seriously with few. The thing done
is handed down; occasionally the name is append-
ed; rarely the actual man who did the thing. One
of the exceptions is Joseph. For while it laughed
at the new king, it kept its eye upon the former
prime minister. Usually, however, in its sardonic
playfulness,

> "Fame is a bee,
>   It has a sting,
>   Ah, too, it has a wing."

A Few Days in Bed

I F your life is crowded, and the doctor orders you to bed, consider yourself fortunate. You will not at the time view the doctor's order in any such favorable light. On the contrary, you will rebel and yield reluctantly. It will seem to you a misfortune and necessary evil. Still, if having gone to bed, you make the best of the situation, it is possible for you to have one of the most rewarding experiences of your life, as many a man can testify.

I have a friend who is a prominent lawyer. He ruefully remarked that he was entering a hospital the next morning. His trouble, so he assured me, was not serious and needed only a minor operation. But he would be in bed for two weeks and so absent from his office for that length of time. This seemed to him a misfortune. Instead of offering sympathy, I congratulated him. Observing his surprise, I asked him to send me a message when he left the hospital. At the end of two weeks came a telegram saying, "Had a wonderful time. You were right."

He went to bed under favorable conditions. His physician advised an operation and a period of rest, promising that he would leave the hospital in better health than he had enjoyed for years. Because of this, he went to bed hopefully. Also, he remained in bed with a clear conscience. He was not seeking a loafer's paradise, as too many men have, to their undoing. Rather, he had temporarily laid aside his work believing that later he would better do his work.

Being in bed for two weeks, this keen and active lawyer had as he said, "a wonderful time." His body relaxed and his mind worked with unaccustomed freedom. Along the pathway of memory he wandered back into the forgotten years and recalled many an experience of other days. To his surprise new ideas and old ideas in more vivid form came to him. For it is a fact of history that in bed some of the great ideas have come to men. For example, the idea of the block system used on the railroads came to the inventor in a period of convalescence.

When this lawyer went to bed, as he told me later, he took with him a problem that he had been unable to solve. As he lay in bed during the enforced leisure, the solution came. His experience was similar to that of Disraeli who said to his wife, "I think that this is the moment to imitate Talleyrand, who, when he could not see very clearly what ought to be done, took to his bed."

More important still, having the leisure and being necessarily detached from the usual routine of his office, this lawyer took a fresh inventory of his own life. Doing this, he discovered the need of some revaluations. His relation to God, to the dear ones in the family circle, and to his fellow men in the ordinary commerce of life, was reexamined. When the time came to leave the hospital and return to his work he did so with a determination not to overlook the things that are more excellent.

If such was his experience, and I have only hinted at the change wrought in his life, then he discovered the beauty and the depth of the Psalmist's words, "The Eternal sustains him on his sick bed and brings him back to health"—health mental and spiritual, as well as physical.

So, if ordered to bed, consider yourself fortunate. It may mean a turning point in your life, as it has in the life of many another busy man. For perhaps you are numbered among those who look up only when flat on their backs.

George Washington and Parson Weems

PARSON Weems has not been treated fairly. The critics have been having a merry time whacking him as an itinerant preacher, fiddler, peddler of his own books. Derisively he has been pictured as inventing the rather wooden story of George Washington and the cherry tree.

But a change is taking place. The stature of this eccentric, lovable and picturesque father of 12 children is growing. The reason is the appearance during the year of an exhaustive study, entitled "Marian Locke Weems, His Works and Ways." It was begun by Paul Leicester Ford who died in 1902. Then the study was completed by Ford's sister, Mrs. Skeel. There are three volumes, and the edition is limited to 300 copies—these placed in the larger libraries.

An examination of the volumes shows that Weems had a flair for journalistic history. Everything he wrote is incurably interesting. Our present-day biographers seek to write so interestingly that their books will become best sellers. From the standpoint of arresting attention Weems has such writers as Emil Ludwig, Bernard Fay, Antoine Maurois and Gamaliel Bradford beaten a mile. His book on Washington has gone through 81 editions, the last three editions since 1900—a hundred years after the first edition. Would anyone dare to suggest that 100 years from now three more editions will be called for of anything written by our modern biographers?

Another thing to notice is that his work has positive value. The historian knows that about the most difficult thing to do is to capture for the written page the folk lore of a period. Weems does this for the Revolutionary period. Our modern biographers are outclassed. They examine documents, and while their writings are interesting and sometimes penetrating, the flavor, as it were, of the soil is lacking. Instead of fingering documents, this genial old parson tarried in taverns and mingled with courthouse crowds. The result is genuine folk lore.

One thing more. The scholarly work mentioned above indicates that Weems was honest. It has been the fashion of our clever historical students to poke fun at the Parson because of his clumsy invention of the cherry tree story. Adopting the argument from silence, they have proven to their own satisfaction that inasmuch as Weems' life of Washington was the first written, and that as he alone among the early writers mentions the story, therefore it was a creation of his own imagination.

But a pottery mug has been discovered in Germany, belonging to the 18th century. On it is the inscription, "G. W. 1776." Also there is a figure with the uniform and cockade hat of an officer of the Continental army. And in the foreground is a hacked cherry tree. The presumption is that the story of the cherry tree was carried back to Germany by a Hessian, and given pictorial representation on a mug of German manufacture. This is the conclusion reached by Mrs. Skeel, one of the joint authors of the book. If so, Parson Weems did not invent the story when he wrote his life of Washington in 1800. Instead he used the story as part of the folk lore about the great hero. Which means that the laugh is on the critics, and not on the really clever Weems.

One of the Two Greatest Achievements

NOTICE that this article has to do with one of the two greatest achievements, not with one of the great achievements. Men have done marvelous things. The discovery that a fallen log, if hollowed out, would float; that by rubbing stones or bits of wood, fire could be made and food cooked: these were wonderful achievements.

Some of the inventions of men have been great. The invention of the alphabet and numerals; of measurement by rules of trigonometry; of the mariner's compass; of the printing press and of the steam engine.

Then men have accomplished amazing things in the arts. The Venus de Milo in sculpture; the Mona Lisa in painting; the Fifth Symphony in music and the Faust or King Lear in writing.

But there are two achievements greater than any mentioned. One, the creation in words of a program for society so perfect that it remains unmodified after the passing of centuries. The credit for this belongs to Jesus, who made the astounding assertion that His program in its wording would never become obsolete. For He said, "But My words will never pass away."

To understand how stupendous this claim as made by Jesus is, you have only to compare His program for society with the famous historic pro-

grams as offered by the great thinkers of the race,
such as Plato, Harrington, Hobbes or More. For
example, read the two programs most often quoted,
those of Plato in the New Republic and More in
Utopia. You will find in each much that is profound and that anticipates our modern needs. But
you also will find much that is as worthless as
decayed branches on a tree.

Not so with the program of Jesus. Men may
neglect His program. Men may attempt a compromise by accepting a part and rejecting a part,
seeking to hide the compromise in words about the
simple gospel as distinct from the social gospel.
Here and there a cynical writer like H. L. Menc-
ken in his latest book, "Treatise on the Gods," or
less penetrating writers like Harry Elmer Barnes,
in his last book, "The Twilight of Christianity,"
may conceitedly think they have moved beyond
the teachings of Jesus. But the more thoughtful
and practical men, who interpret life not through
books but through life itself, know that the Man
of Galilee is generations ahead of us, and that the
task of this generation is to move forward and
practice what He taught.

Whenever the water in the pool of society be-
gins to stir as indicative of a desire for a better
world, we instinctively begin to quote the gospel
of Jesus. This is so, because the seminal thoughts
for human progress are always found in His gospel. Such noble ideals as an equitable distribution
of wealth, equality before the law, human worth
based upon character, freedom of conscience, dig-

nity of honest labor, and a warless world, harmonize with the teachings of Jesus, as the feathers on a partridge blend with the leaves.

That Jesus could give in words a program for society that time cannot touch is the second greatest achievement of history. And the first greatest achievement is that in His own life He faultlessly expressed what in words He so perfectly uttered. His words and His deeds constitute the two supreme accomplishments of mankind—so supreme that they stand forth as two miracles.

Your Children—Their Incidental Education

MOTHERS, exemplary in every other respect, are genial and harmless liars regarding their children.

It is harmless because no one ever believes the mother. What business man would think of hiring a boy on the recommendation of his mother?

This tendency on the part of mothers, to see more in their children than others could possibly see, has always existed. In the Bible we read: "Then children were brought to Him that He might lay His hand on them and pray for them."

These mothers had no knowledge of Jesus based on personal experience. All they knew was the rumor going the rounds that a wonderful teacher had come to town. This was enough for them. Their children must have the hand of this marvelous prophet rest upon their heads, and hear His voice in a word of prayer uttered over them. And, of course, there would be no difficulty in arranging for this. In fact, the mothers suspected that the new teacher would feel honored in having their budding young geniuses presented to him.

All this is naive and beautiful, if a bit amusing on the part of the mothers. But as you consider the situation carefully you also discover something very shrewd. They evidently believed that the momentary contact of their children with this remarkable man would have an educational value. In years to come it would be a wonderful thing, so they believed, for their children to look back and say that upon a certain day and in a certain place, the hand of Jesus for one brief moment actually rested upon their heads. In acting upon this belief these Jewish mothers practiced sound pedagogy.

For there is educational value in the brief glimpse which a child is privileged to have of an exceptional person. Give your child the best in the school; also, encourage the child in the reading of good books. But in addition, and especially while the child is young, provide an occasional glimpse. When the finished artist, the great orator or the famous traveler comes to town, if possible, arrange for your child to see the distinguished person. Many an abiding interest in art, music, travel or some worthy cause, owes its beginning to a momentary glimpse in the earlier years.

From a slightly different angle the same thought is expressed in the remark which one of our great university presidents made to me some years ago. He said that when his children were young he always welcomed the opportunity of entertaining in his home, if only for a meal or over night, some missionary from the foreign field. The stalwart character of a person devoting his life unselfishly to a cause, together with the fund of unusual information about a distant part of the world, so he believed, had an educational value for his children.

And this famous educator of a generation ago

was right. For today of his three children, one is a leading lawyer, a second is the wife of a celebrated scholar, and the third is the president of a famous university that ranks second to none in America. Yes, there is educational value in the passing glimpse.

The Book Everyone Should Know

THE Bible as we have it today is a library of sixty-six books—books of prose, poetry, proverbs, narratives, prophesies, letters, and histories. When the Psalmist lived the library was being formed. Yet with only a portion of it in existence he said, "Thy word is a lamp unto my feet, and a light unto my path."

He knew his Bible. Only a man who had read and reread its pages could speak of it as a lamp and a light. Had he heard of someone writing about "The Book That Nobody Knows," he would have been surprised. But he lived before the days of advertising.

Today, people are reading the Bible to improve their language as spoken and written. This need of better English is in the air. Magazines carry announcements of short cuts to a mastery of the English language. But these schemes have little worth. As the biological value of play is in playing and not in being played to, so the cultural value of language is not in reading about good English, but in reading the English. That is, read your Bible until your mind comes up dripping with its words.

A boy left home with the education of a country school. Later, he decided to devote his life to religious work. With his Bible he began. Years went by and he found himself giving a series of talks with Gladstone among his hearers. After the last address the statesman said that he had been listening to the purest English since John Bunyon. The speaker, Moody, had soaked his mind in the language of the Bible.

Thoughtful people are reading the Bible in their search for a deeper meaning of life.

Psychology is a word to conjure with at the present time. In education its tendency on the whole seems to be inimical to religion. I have a cultured, broad-minded friend who is the president of a college with about two thousand students. Its traditions are religious. He tells me that for two years he has been searching for a scholarly young man with enough religion to make it safe to turn him loose as a teacher of psychology. And he has not found him.

A reading of the Bible will serve as a corrective to this tendency. For it contains more sound psychology than is found in all the books written on the subject, including the masterpieces by William James and G. Stanley Hall—who are in a measure out of date.

Again, the Bible is being read by many because it gives an added zest to their lives. Sometimes a tonic for the body is needed; more often for the mind. Most of us work in a restricted field of interests. The conditions under which we live tend to become commonplace. To overcome these restricted interests and commonplace conditions, many a man has turned to the exhilarating mental tonic of the Bible, taking a small dose each day.

To change the figure, Henry Ward Beecher had a jeweller friend who would loan him a few gems, which he would carry about and enjoy in moments of quiet. In the Bible there are great thoughts which are as jewels of priceless value. It is our privilege to carry them about with us and delight in them while from their facets iridescent colors of truth flash beauty into our lives.

Such are some of the values in a fairly constant reading of the Bible. A cleansing and strengthening of our language; a deepening of our thoughts about personality; and a freshening of our outlook upon life. Because of these values no sensible man can afford to omit the Bible from his program of living.

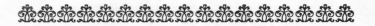

Big Stick, Yardstick, and Candlestick

FOR generations unnumbered the big stick was lustily swung. As civilization became less crude the swinging was more adroitly done. Kings placed crowns upon their heads and ruled by divine right. Battle captains engaged in military aggression because war is a biological necessity. Industrial leaders controlled labor markets on the basis of economic equilibrium. Still, these words about divine right, biological necessity, and economic equilibrium were only euphemisms to hide the swinging of the big stick.

It may be assumed that in times past the big stick was necessary. Moreover let us grant that under present conditions the big stick cannot be altogether dispensed with. As Mrs. Browning says:

> Children use the fist, until they are of age
> To use the brain,
> And so we needed Caesar's to assist
> Man's justice, and Napoleon's to explain
> God's counsel.

But the big stick is being replaced by the yardstick. The distinctive contribution of this age of science is the method of measurement. As never before intelligent men are laying the yardstick on the things of life and seeking to guide their acts by facts. The expression of the change that has come over the modern world is found in the familiar remark of Herbert Spencer that a tragedy is an hypothesis killed by a fact.

This remarkable increase in the use of the yardstick, to be sure, is resented. There is nothing more futile or amusing than the existence of rear admirals lounging in the easy chairs of their clubs and swinging their verbal big sticks in support of theories that belong to a day that has past. They remind us of the famous colored preacher Brother Jaspar who insisted upon preaching that the sun do move.

Nevertheless, the yardstick is not enough. The marvels of measurement may be cheerfully granted. But the very success of the method is our peril. For the table of life is groaning with the food of facts. Because of this, the danger that confronts us is that of mental indigestion due to our failure to absorb and understand the stupendous mass of facts assembled. Like the cannon at Balaklava, facts are to the right of us, to the left of us, in front of us, behind us, and thundering at us. The average man today is bewildered.

If the big stick has been swung, the yardstick laid, the candlestick needs to be held. Compelling force has gradually given way to indubitable facts. Now these facts must be supplemented by penetrating insight. Not less of science but more of philosophy is the demand of the hour. That is, men who can accept and put into the practice the words of the Apostle when he exhorts his hearers to "Think on these things."

You remember that Charles Lamb, having listened to a disparagement of Shakespeare, took a lighted candle from the mantel, and approaching the person who had been talking, asked the privilege of examining his brain. So with the facts being accumulated by the yardstick method. They need to be examined in the light of the candlestick of truth. Only as this is done is progress possible.

Laughter Above the Clouds

TURNING the pages of your Bible you come upon these words, "He that sitteth in the heavens will laugh." Read in connection with the verses that go before, the strange words indicate that God laughs at man. To conceive of the Sovereign One enthroned high in the heavens and laughing at us is somewhat disconcerting, even humiliating.

If God laughs at us it is reasonable to assume that He needs laughter. Our knowledge of the Most High is based upon what we know about ourselves. In our finite lives laughter is as normal as tears. This leads to the belief that laughter is natural to the infinite personality of God.

Life seen as grotesque, as all of us know from experience, is the food upon which laughter feeds. To use the old Greek expression, it is life humorously perceived as a cow jumping over the moon —head down, tail out, and shooting through space. Laughter itself is outward manifestation in voice or eye—the most subtle form of laughter is with the eye—of which humor is the inner quality.

Man himself, let us with bowed heads admit, furnishes the food, for man alone is grotesque. Inanimate things are sometimes queer—the gnarled trunk of a tree or the weird formation of a rock. Animals are often amusing—a dog chasing its tail or a kitten playing with a ball of yarn. But man

49

is the only thing in creation that is cause for shattering laughter. For he is the only thing big enough to make a big fool of himself. Therefore, if God laughs, the laughter is called forth by man.

To conceive of God laughing at us, leads to the inference that the grotesque is fundamental in life. To state it in another way, life is a shield. Viewed from one side it is somber and serious; from the other side it is incongruous and grotesque. Evidence for this abounds on every hand.

Consider the fact that tears and laughter are near together in our lives. The orator who can start tears can as easily stir laughter. Like the sunshine and the rain in the same field during the April shower, tears and laughter are almost blended in our lives. As Oliver Wendell Holmes reminds us, tears are the water power and laughter the wind power which turns the machinery of life.

Glance at Shakespeare. In his tragedies he interprets life as serious; in his comedies as grotesque. For generations young people in their debating societies have discussed the question whether the tragedies or the comedies give us the deeper insight into life. Today they are no nearer answering the question than they were generations ago. For it is "six of one and half a dozen of the other."

Think for a moment of the cartoon. At its best it is a form of art. As comedy states the grotesque in terms of literature, so the cartoon states it in terms of art. The effectiveness of the cartoon is in its ability to portray life as a cow jumping over the moon. How effective it can be is seen when we recall that Nast's cartoons sent the members of the Tweed Ring to prison.

Laughter can be terribly effective. And awed and reverently we think of God seated upon his throne in the heavens above the clouds, at times laughing at his offspring.

The Sermon on the Mount and the Supreme Court

IF there are verses in the Bible that like jewels flash from their facets iridescent colors of truth, there are extended portions that like pieces of jewelry are set with many gems and create ensemble effects. One such is the Sermon on the Mount.

To understand the modern world this document should be known. The recent decision of the Supreme court in the Rosika Schwimmer case makes this clear.

By a vote of six to three this woman's request for citizenship was denied. The question of physical, mental, or moral fitness was not raised. Devotion to our government as coming nearest her ideal of a democratic republic was granted. Being a woman, it was assumed that she would never shoulder a gun. But her declaration that in the event of war she would refuse to bear arms, would, so the court held, have a deterrent influence upon others as regards the defensive clause in the naturalization act of 1916. Therefore, no citizenship.

In the minority opinion, Mr. Justice Holmes mentions the Quakers and says that he had not supposed "hitherto that we regretted our inability to expel them because they believe more than some of us do in the teachings of the Sermon on the Mount."

These words are interesting as coming from the only member of the court who has experienced war. Those familiar with the writings of Oliver Wendell Holmes, will recall the allusions to his boy in the Union Army. This boy is now the learned and venerable justice who writes these words.

Doubtless, had one stood near enough to catch the modulation in the voice and the twinkle in the eye, when the words about the Quakers and the Sermon on the Mount were read, he would have detected either a play of gentle humor or a bit of subtle irony.

Still the question is, Just what is in the mind of the famous jurist in using these words? Would he suggest that the Quakers are mistaken in basing their doctrine of non-resistance upon the Sermon on the Mount! Or, would he intimate that if men had courage enough to accept the teachings of the Sermon wars would cease?

In seeking an answer to these questions, let us do two things: One is, read the majority and minority opinions in this memorable case. There are no legal technicalities to obscure the reasoning. The arguments are clearly presented and stated in robust Anglo-Saxon that any layman of average intelligence can easily follow.

The other is, devote half an hour to reading the Sermon on the Mount. It is among the most vital utterances of history, and in our modern world is more often quoted than any other document in existence. To read these words of the Spiritual Genius of the race is a dangerous procedure. For you may find yourself swinging in thought even beyond Justice Holmes and agreeing with the Quakers. At least, reacting to the thoughts expressed on the hill top in the long ago you will become a more thoughtful citizen—and thought is at a premium in America today.

Cleopatra's Nose—Its Problem

WHAT gives to history its fascination, and at the same time makes so baffling its final meaning, is the element of contingency. Our historians, borrowing the phrase from Pascal, call the existence of the element of contingency the problem of Cleopatra's nose.

By this is meant that had the nose of this famous woman been a fraction of an inch longer or shorter, the course of the Roman Empire would have been otherwise. For the influence which she exerted over the Roman leaders was due in a measure to her physical beauty. Having a nose too small or too large she would have lacked the ravishing beauty, and so would have been unable to charm Julius Caesar, Mark Antony, and other susceptible gentlemen.

This element of contingency that baffles the historical student is found in the Bible. For example, it is found in the story of Joseph who as a lad left his home in Judea and in time became Prime Minister of Egypt. You recall the words in the opening portion of this matchless biography—"And behold, a caravan of Israelites was coming from the Gilead." These words seem incidental enough. But the appearance of this caravan was to Joseph and his brothers what the nose of Cleopatra was to those coming under her sway. Had the caravan not appeared just when it did, the story of

Joseph, likewise the history of Egypt would have been different. The slave traders coming upon the scene at a particular moment changed the direction of events and made possible a remarkable career.

To understand this, remember that the lad Joseph had aroused the envious opposition of his older brothers. This became so bitter that they threw the boy into an empty cistern to starve to death, and then with cruel contentment they sat down to eat their midday meal. But unexpectedly the caravan appears and the thought comes into their minds of selling the lad to these slave dealers. So the boy is hauled up from the cistern and disappears with the caravan.

In the slave mart of the distant land Joseph attracts the attention of Potiphar, who buys him for the king. Being exceptional in character and ability, this gives the young Hebrew his opportunity. Through the vicissitudes of an eventful career he moves steadily forward and at last becomes prime minister of Egypt.

Here is a perfect illustration of the Cleopatra nose problem as it is presented in the history of nations, the rise of movements, and the experience of individuals inconspicuous no less than conspicuous. What is the solution of this problem? How explain the appearance of the caravan at just the opportune moment?

If we could confine our thought to this particular event it would be easy to reach the conclusion that the hand of God is in the affairs of men. For the coming upon the scene of the slave traders saved the life of Joseph, sent him away to Egypt, and gave him a chance to climb to a position of power. But alas this element of contingency is a two-edged sword that cuts both ways. A fog setting in, the Pilgrim Fathers lost their direction and landed on Cape Cod, thus making possible the history of New England. But a floating iceberg sent the *Titanic* to the bottom of the ocean. Which event will you choose? A chance word gave a young man a suggestion which sent him forward on a successful career. A hidden germ in the glass of milk lodged in the body of another young man and sent him to an early grave. Are the lives of both young men in the plan of God? Here is something of a problem. Do not be in a hurry to solve it. For fools rush in where angels fear to tread.

Cisterns and Wells

NO book equals the Bible in its use of metaphors. These, if brought together, would constitute a noble philosophy of life. Such a grouping would include these words: "Therefore with joy shall ye draw water out of the wells of salvation."

A metaphor suggests rather than defines. This one suggests the contrast between drawing from a cistern and drawing from a well. The water in a cistern is stagnant; its quantity is measurable; and usually it is surface water. There is no joy in hauling water out of a cistern. With a well it is otherwise. The water is alive; it comes from springs that feed the well; and these springs are deep down. To draw water out of a well is a joy.

So with life. The question is whether to draw with joy from wells down deep in ourselves, or without joy from cisterns outside of ourselves. That is, whether life will be conventional and regulatory or vital and expansive.

Phillips Brooks in writing to his brother mentioned the presence of some Harvard students. Then he added: "Their religion does not seem to have harmed them." The sting of this comment is in the inference that religion can harm people. This sting is sharpened by the fact that the inference is true. For religion with some people results in the ingrowing pains of an uncomfortable disposition, instead of the outgoing strength of a joyous freedom. The reason is they are drawing from cisterns rather than wells.

The value of joy is that it is ours when most needed. The water being down deep in our lives, the supply is unfailing. So, there is always the joy of drawing. This is a beautiful and no less profound truth. To state it in another way, joy is a quality of life that exists independently of many things that we possess or fail to possess.

All of us desire health. Yet to have health does not insure joy, and the absence of health does not preclude joy. I lift my hat each morning to a sweet little woman with wasted body who sits in an invalid's chair by the window, and whose answering smile of joy starts the bells ringing in my soul.

Most of us want wealth, for it is a form of power and all normal persons long for power. But the amount of joy does not necessarily increase as you pass from the cottage to the mansion. Sometimes there is more joy in the cottage than in the mansion; again, more joy in the mansion than the cottage.

Some of us seek fame. To aim at achievement exceptional enough to justify the attention of others is not unworthy, if the emphasis be placed upon the achievement and not upon the attention. There are those who secure the fame and retain the joy. Still there are many whose names never reach the front pages of newspapers who have found the secret of a vibrant joy.

But let us not indulge in a false simplicity. In order to have wells from which we may draw, the wells must be dug. This we do with the spade of experience. For joy is the result of a conscious and positive effort in reaching down into the deeper meaning of life.

Perhaps the Greatest Discovery

MONCURE D. CONWAY, in conversation with John Stuart Mill, told how as a young man he was walking along a road in Virginia with a copy of Emerson under his arm. Coming to a cool spot in the shade of a tree by the side of the road he sat down to rest. While sitting there he casually opened the volume of the Concord sage and read a sentence that changed his outlook upon life. The great English thinker hearing of this experience remarked, "Young man, return at once to America and rear a monument where the new conception of life came to you."

In the Bible is a simple statement of fact in ten words as follows: "Then began men to call upon the name of Jehovah." Who the men were and where they lived is not known. If the spot could be located, representatives of the nations of the earth might well assemble and dedicate a monument to the memory of these unknown men. For they made a discovery, perhaps the greatest discovery in the life of mankind.

As suggestive of the import of these few words notice that history is a record of human experience. It is no longer the account of kings and battle captains, but the story of civilization. And civilization is man's achievement in adjusting himself to his environment. In making this adjustment, he has made one discovery after another.

"Then began men to"—use fire, to shape fish hooks, to hollow out logs and float them, to make tents, to fashion harp and pipe, to forge metal tools, to draw lines called letters and group them in an alphabet, to set a needle in straw for a compass, to cast movable type in a mold, to harness steam and electricity, and so on down to our technological age with science working overtime to ferret out new secrets.

But there is another wording. "Then began men to call upon the name of Jehovah." This along with fire, fish hooks and other things, belongs in the story of civilization. For man's environment to which he increasingly adjusts himself is psychical as well as physical. Because of this, an adequate telling of the story must include man in relation to God, no less than man in relation to Nature.

For a time came when men discovered a power outside of themselves as actual as the power in fire, air and water. This use of power they called prayer. Later, the symbol for this power they expressed in their temples.

So the story of civilization has to do with man a religious being, quite as much as man a physical being. As he has modified but not outgrown his early physical discoveries, so, also, he has not gone beyond his need of prayer. The last ocean liner may be a marked improvement over the first log used as a canoe. Yet, both are conditioned upon the fact that they can float.

Primitive and modern man differ much in their

outlook upon life. But regardless of this difference their soul hunger remains the same. Early
man felt the need of help more than human. In
the urge of this need he discovered an unseen,
mysterious energy at his disposal. His use of
this energy he called prayer. Modern man does
the same. He knows that to be at his best means
that he must draw upon every resource within
reach. One such resource is spiritual energy. To
draw upon this is to call upon the name of Jehovah.

Aground on the Mud Flats

TOO much fair weather becomes monotonous. Grey atmosphere, hanging mist, and wet clouds are needed. What the shifting winds and overcast skies are to nature, changing moods are to human nature. Among these moods the most extreme and dangerous is the mood of despondency. When this mood becomes dominant life is on the mud flats with the tide running out. But this mood of despondency has its variations.

Surprising as it is, there are people who deliberately anchor their skiffs on the mud flats. Being the victims of an inverted egotism, they seek the luxury of a sigh. They encourage the mood of despondency, the psychiatrists tell us, in order to capture a sense of importance.

Some reach the flats through a failure to heed the buoys in the channel of right living. The tide being high the mud flats were hidden. They forgot the morning after. Now, the reaction having set in, they are aground in the shallow water of a bitter despondency—remorse.

Others have drifted on to the flats. These people need a sensible minister plus a physician with a knowledge of psychotherapeutics. For the moment they are micro-depressives, to use Overstreet's term. But the keels of their craft may become embedded in the mud—then a mental hospital.

Many are on the flats for a brief time. During the afternoon the sky was clear and the air crisp. With night the fog shut in, an ebb tide began to flow, and losing their bearings they went aground. But with turn of tide and lifting of fog they will soon be afloat. This is temperamental despondency—swift and shattering while it lasts, and the kind that high strung, sensitive, and exceptional characters yield to.

Elijah the prophet was aground under these conditions when he wailed out, "It is enough, now, O Jehovah, take my life, for I am not better than my fathers." Surely, he was on the mud flats.

But the great man was utterly exhausted. Under intense strain he had stood on a mountain through the hours of the day, and raced in a wild wind and rain storm beside a chariot during the hours of the night. Doubling on his tracks he had in fear traveled many miles. He was physically worn out and needed sleep and food. Along with his body his mind was tired. And the mind behaves queerly as it reacts to a fatigued body. Moreover, he was in the grip of an enforced inactivity. This effected him even more than his exhausted body and weary mind. For men go to pieces many times when compelled to be still.

Under these conditions a sense of utter loneliness came to him. This is a sign of this type of despondency. One greater than Elijah asked God why He had forsaken Him. And stranger still, a feeling of irretrievable failure swept over him. Another indication of being on the mud flats of despondency.

In August, 1864, Abraham Lincoln showed to members of his cabinet a sealed envelope, which was to be opened on a specified day. He believed the people had deserted him and the cause was lost. In the envelope were suggestions to his successor in office. In November, 1864, he was triumphantly reelected. For a brief period like Elijah he was on the mud flats of despondency, with a cold, wet wind blowing. But the tide turned, the wind shifted, the mud flats became submerged, and his craft floated off into deepwater.

Floating the Craft into Deeper Water

A STRONG man having yielded to a mood of deep despondency, as strong men sometimes do, is like a huge ship having grounded on the mud flats with the tide running out. Each for the time being is an impressive embodiment of helplessness—the helplessness emphasized by the bigness of the life and the hugeness of the ship. Each needs help. For each is in such a predicament that assistance must come from without itself.

With the ship help will come from the energy of the incoming tide. Its supply of fuel may be abundant, and its engines oiled, perfectly geared, and powerful. Other craft may be hovering near eager to throw a line. But these things are of no avail. Not until the tide turns and flowing in lifts the keel of the huge ship clear of the mud bottom have these other sources of power any value.

So with a human life that has gone aground on the mud flats of temporary despondency. At the moment the life can do little for itself and other lives can do less. To urge the victim to brace up, or to offer the victim your sympathy is futile. The first need is the omnipotent power of God expressed in the energy of nature. This is finely shown in the experience of Elijah under the juniper tree when in a mood of utter despondency he moaned forth the words, "It is enough, now, O Jehovah, take my life, for I am not better than my fathers."

He is so despondent that he wants to die. Fortunately, he is exhausted physically. Soon he falls asleep. As he lies upon the ground and the hours silently pass, the invisible energy of God in the form of sleep flows into his tired body, like the tide coming in from the deep.

> The innocent sleep.
> Sleep that knits up the ravelled sleeve of care,
> The death of each day's life, sore nature's bath.

Later he awakens and at his head is a fire burning, some bread having been baked, and a jug of water. Being hungry he eats of the bread. And again the energy of God in the form of food flows in like the incoming tide.

Then refreshed by sleep and strengthened by food he arises and goes on a journey to Horeb the historic mountain. Still more energy flows in. This time it is mental and spiritual in the form of ennobling memories. For he is in the region in which Moses tarried when he received from God the Ten Commandments.

This all appears so simple—almost too simple to be true. To think of energy in the form of sleep, food and memory lifting a man out of his despondency and sending him forth to live a normal life. But the quiet, incoming tide of the ocean will lift a trans-atlantic liner that is aground and send it on its way between continents.

Also, it may seem humiliating to make so much of energy that flows in from without, and so little of our own effort. But this is true in life. In the growing of a bushel of wheat less than ten per cent is the result of man's effort and more than 90 per cent is due to nature—soil, air, wind and sunlight.

Perhaps the secret of strong living is to place ourselves in such a position as to utilize advantageously the energy at our disposal. In other words, to be in tune with the Infinite. If an experience with despondency teaches us this, it will not be an unmixed evil.

Hindenburg the Hero of the People

THE most picturesque man in public life, who comes nearest being the cynosure of the civilized world, is the old man, 82 years of age, Paul Hindenburg, President of the German Republic. Evidence for this is an avid public that is reading everything about him in the books and magazines.

How explain this? Unlike Bismarck he is not a man of ideas. He has no theory of economics as has President Hoover. He possesses no flair for politics as do Aristide Briand and Ramsay MacDonald. On the contrary, a reading of his Memoirs indicates a positive dislike for politics. Yet he is the most popular figure in Germany and the most interesting character to the reading public of the world at large.

The explanation is in two words—imagination and character. Asquith, in his recent work, "Fifty Years of British Parliament," reminds us that in the 19th century Disraeli appealed to the imagination and Gladstone to the conscience of the English people. Hindenburg in the 20th century appeals both to the imagination and the conscience of the people.

He is a soldier, not a statesman. The active years have been spent in the army. Through disagreement with his Kaiser he withdraws from

active service. At 67, in the crisis of the World
War he again unsheathes his sword and smashing
the Russian army in the East he becomes the
"Grand old man of the lakes." As the war ends
in defeat, and while the Kaiser is ignominiously
seeking safety in a neutral country, he remains at
his post of duty and receives the tired and battered
troops returning from the horrors of the trenches.
At 77, he is dragged from his retirement at Han-
over, and to the surprise of the world is elected
the President of the German Republic. Yes, the
imagination is kindled as this grim old man whose
hand has always grasped the sword is now visual-
ized as holding the pen.

But if he kindles the imagination, he even more
appeals to the conscience. And to appeal to the
conscience is to reach deeper than to kindle the
imagination. Recall your feelings when the cable
flashed the news in 1925 that Hindenburg had
been elected the second President of the Republic.
Your reaction was one of disappointment as you
felt that his election meant a return of the dreaded
and discredited monarchy. If my memory be
trustworthy, a shudder of fear passed over the
forward-looking people of the world.

Yet the thing so many thought might happen
is precisely the thing that has not happened. As
Dr. Leder, editor of the *Tageblatt* of Berlin, said
to me recently, Erbert, a Socialist and the first
President of the Republic, stabilized capital;
Hindenburg, a monarchist and the second President, stabilized the Republic. This is a striking

but accurate statement of the situation. And the editor added, because of Hindenburg's course of action since becoming President, probably 95 per cent of the people in Germany are today devoted to the Republic.

Still the question remains, How account for the influence exercised by this old soldier with few ideas, little of economic theory, and no flair for politics? And, remember, it is an influence exerted in a direction the opposite of his own convictions. For there can be no doubt that in his heart Hindenburg believes in the monarchy. Yet he stabilizes the Republic. What is the answer? It is that Hindenburg upon becoming President took seriously his oath to support the Republic. He is old-fashioned enough to believe in God, the Ten Commandments and the sacredness of his word. Like Job in the Bible he has said, "Till I die, I will not put away mine integrity from me." Here is the secret of his hold upon the people.

Throwing Bridges across Streams

THE water of the lake in the mountains may be so still and clear that its depth can be missed. In the Bible there are words so few and simple that their profound implication can be overlooked. Such are the words, "And God said, Let the earth put forth grass." Using less than a dozen monosyllables a stupendous problem is stated—the problem of a mysterious transition in nature. These transitions have been three in number: From the non-living to the living—the plant; from the living to the conscious—the animal; and from the conscious to the self-conscious—the human. The nine crisp words quoted above deal with the first of these transitions and suggest the question, Why?

A partial answer is, that vegetation came by utilizing elements at a lower level—sunlight, air, rain, and soil. Like throwing a pontoon bridge across a stream by using material gathered on the bank, so in moving from the non-living to the living, material on the shore of the non-living was used.

Something new appeared. The engineer in throwing his bridge over the stream uses the timber on the shore; also, something more. So, in addition to sunlight, air, rain, and soil, something with a capacity to grow from within out appeared.

Until the first tiny blade of grass lifted its head above the earth there was no growth, only increase in size due to accretion.

But the big, fascinating question that is haunting the scientists in the laboratories today, and which remains unanswered is this: Did the first blade of grass come as a development at a higher level— the living, of that which was implicit at a lower level—the non-living? Or did something not found at the lower level enter, in order to make possible life at a higher level? In other words, where did the something more than the timber used by the engineer in throwing his bridge across the stream come from? This is the stupendous problem of the origin of life.

Some scientists have balked at the idea of the vital being the product of the non-vital. So they have indulged in the weird speculation regarding germs of life borne in the crevices of meteorites or wafted by light waves amid cosmic dust, and by chance coming to the earth. Hence the blade of grass.

Other scientists in the grip of the evolutionary theory make the hurdle of the seemingly impossible, and believe that as a result of chemical reactions life is the product of non-life. In fact, a few years ago, the wine of the development idea having gone to the heads of some scientists, the statement was made that the origin of life had been discovered in the ooze at the bottom of the sea. But the "morning after" came, and only the ooze was left.

Still the dream of discovering the process persists. Some day it may be realized. Should the origin of life be experimentally established, would God be ruled out? No. For only an engineer of infinite intelligence—God, could assemble the material on the bank for the pontoon bridge across the stream of creation, over which the vital could pass to the other bank of things that grow. Religion has nothing to fear from science, and science has nothing to fear from religion. For they are handmaidens serving in the temple of the Sovereign God.

Teachers, Preachers, and Statesmen

THE able political writer, Clinton W. Gilbert, in a recent article stated the position of Dwight W. Morrow on the liquor problem. This citizen, who has suddenly loomed large on the horizon of public life, is presented as believing that the use of liquor is a personal question. The function of government "ends with the regulation of the manufacture of alcoholic drinks and of the condition of their sale."

This does not mean that Mr. Morrow favors the use of alcoholic liquor. On the contrary, it is probable that he sees in its use an evil and would welcome its disappearance from society. But the government has nothing to do with its disappearance. This is a moral problem to be solved by the individual. The task of government is limited to regulation and sale. This, of course, is harking back to the license system, whether the thing licensed is the saloon or some new form of organization.

What especially interested me in this presentation, however, was the high esteem in which this banker and diplomatist holds the church and the school. To quote: "That is why the prohibition problem will not be solved until the teachers and preachers see it clearly." The problem is moral and personal, therefore, the solution rests with teachers and preachers. With this thought I am in entire accord. The individual aspect of prohibition and the responsibility of preachers and teachers cannot be emphasized too strongly.

In doing so, two facts need to be kept in mind. One is, that for many years teachers and preachers have recognized their responsibility. The splendid advance registered during the past fifty years in dealing with the liquor traffic, is due mainly to the church and school. Those who favor alcoholic drinks may think it wise to exaggerate the importance of the Anti-Saloon League as a semi-political organization. But those of us who have been on the firing line for more than a generation, know that such exaggeration is dishonest. Progress has been made because of the moral awakening of the church as regards the devastating social effect of strong drink, and the quiet foundation work of the schools in teaching scientific temperance, that is, the reaction of the human body to alcohol as a poison.

The other fact is, that a moral question when its social implications are so clearly perceived that a preponderant body of public opinion is created, tends inevitably to pass into law. Justice is a moral and personal question with social ramifications, hence the prohibition in the law against certain forms of injustice. Integrity is a no less personal and moral question, hence the prohibition against perjury. Sexual purity is moral and personal but with distinct social consequences, hence the prohibition against adultery. Likewise, the use of alcoholic drinks is a moral and personal question, no less so and no more so than the question of justice, sexual purity, and integrity. If those prohibitions in the law that are primarily personal and moral are to be eliminated, then little of vital law will be left.

To return to the teachers and preachers. Because they faithfully and intelligently exercised their influence, the prohibition of the liquor business became the law of the land. And it will remain the law of the land until these representatives of the school and the church are satisfied that the leopard of strong drink has changed its spots and is no longer a social menace—which is unlikely. For as the Bible says, "No one is any use to the Reign of God who puts his hand to the plough and then looks back."

Two Men Talking in a Cabin

JUST a talk.   One man laying aside the duties of office and crossing the Atlantic to be a guest; the other man turning away from governmental routine to be a host.   Both men going to an appointed spot—to talk.   But one man was prime minister of England and the other was President of the United States.   They met as the official heads of the two great English-speaking nations of the world.

The quiet, elevation and beauty of the hills furnished the surroundings for their talk.   To leave behind the imposing Capitol with its Executive Mansion and go to a modest cabin was wise.   It was superb political strategy, for it caught the imagination of the civilized world.   They might pause at the entrance to the cabin on the mountain side and enjoy the panorama of nature in all the glory of her autumnal foliage that unfolded before them.   But standing there, they formed an even more beautiful picture of two strong men having journeyed hither to talk.

Historic memories crowded in upon them as they did their talking.   Draw a circle with a diameter of a hundred miles and the little brown cabin on the mountain side as the center, and within this circle is the most historic region on the continent.   In imagination as they looked forth they saw the homes of famous English country gentlemen who

became loyal American citizens. Within this circle four of the early Presidents of the Republic
were born—George Washington, Thomas Jefferson, James Madison and James Monroe.   Still
within the circle four other men lived who
wrought mightily in the formative period of the
nation—George Mason, Patrick Henry, George
Rogers C ark, and John Marshall. Like the gentle
sound of the Rapidan flowing near the cabin on the
mountain side, the memory of these great men
sounded in their souls as they talked.

But the important thought is that the President
and the prime minister by meeting in the cabin
made history. A generation hence it may be seen
that they perpetuated the noblest traditions of the
past, modified by the changed conditions of the
present. For they talked about safeguarding the
peace of the world through a limitation, and if
possible, a reduction of armaments. Visualize
them in the cool of the October mountain air,
seated before the fireplace in which the logs
burned, as they made history. The warm glow of
the fire encouraged the friendly spirit; the sparks
flying reminded them that in sincerity their minds
must clash as they expressed divergent thoughts;
and the weird shapes and colors of the embers
quickened the almost unbelievable ideal held in
common of a warless world. What a scene for
an artist!

They did their memorable talking on a Sunday,
for they arrived on a Saturday evening and left on
a Monday morning. Being religious men—the

one a Quaker and the other a Scotch Presbyterian,
the Bible probably was mentioned.   If so, were
the following words quoted: "Let Christian wisdom rule your behavior to the outside world; make
the very most of your time; let your talk always
have a saving salt of grace about it, and learn to
answer any question put to you."

Anything New under the Sun?

TO what extent are the following words true? "That which hath been is that which shall be; and that which hath been done, is that which shall be done: and there is nothing new under the sun." Our first reaction is unfavorable. The words have meaning only as they reveal the cloyed spirit of a man who has reached the point where life has become blasé. For things are being done that have never before been done. Novel creations are found on every hand. Certainly the thinkers are not all wrong who tell us that we are living in a new era. Such are some of the thoughts that come to the surface of the mind as these words are read.

Yet this remarkable utterance is in the Bible, and registers the observation of one of the profoundest philosophers of history. Perhaps the best way to test the accuracy of these words is to picture this Oriental thinker, by name, Solomon, returning to life and visiting America. Should he thus return, would he stand by his opinion given centuries ago?

He would be conscious of no change as he gazed upon heaven and earth. For he would see the sky overhead, sun shining, stars twinkling, mountains towering, valleys blossoming, winds blowing, rains falling, and grains growing. It would be the same old world of varied form, sound, and color.

As he observed the basis experiences of human life he would find them as he had known them in the years of his former existence. The mystery of birth at the beginning of the pilgrimage; the equal mystery of death at the end of the pilgrimage; and the elemental needs—food, drink, clothing, and sleep, along the road of the pilgrimage.

Looking about he would marvel at man's inventiveness in using Nature for his own ends. On land, sea, and in the air he would see extensions of man's legs, arms, eyes, ears, and mouth, as based upon steam and electricity. He would perceive, however, that these machines indicate capacity to utilize, not ability to originate.

Being a philosopher, and turning from the machines to man himself, he would make a remarkable discovery. For he would find that whereas man has shown marvelous inventiveness in the use of things, he has shown little ingenuity in the handling of moral forces.

So utterly devoid of originality is man, that he has been unable to invent a single new virtue. He is surprisingly clever with his compass, printing press, steam engine, motor car and aeroplane. Listening to the ministers and priests, this philosopher from the antique world would hear them insisting upon the virtues he dwelt upon in a book he wrote 3000 years ago—love, integrity, loyalty, reverence, purity, industry and unselfishness.

Moreover, man has been unable to invent a

single new sin.　Solomon, in his Book of Proverbs, dealth with the sins of his day, which are precisely the sins we are battling with in America today. If you doubt this, read the book.　Having done so, you will feel that it might be published as the last word on the crime situation in the nation.

Yes, the words of Solomon are true.　But, being true, the conclusion does not follow that there is no such thing as progress.　There are 26 letters in the alphabet and seven primary colors.　Yet undreamed-of things in literature and art are possible with these letters and colors.　So with the virtues of life; alas, also with the sins of life.

The Police of New York and Berlin

THE newspapers announce the appointment by Congress of a commission with Congressman Hamilton Fish as chairman to investigate the Communists of this country. To this commission the following is respectfully submitted.

On the afternoon of May 1, 1929, a sick friend in the Polyclinic hospital on the West Side of New York was visited. Leaving the hospital, police on the opposite side of the street were noticed. Being a stranger in the neighborhood and not a frequenter of prize fights, the imposing building around which the police as a cordon were drawn was not recognized as the new Madison Square Garden. A passer-by informed me that the police were thus in evidence because the Communists were holding their annual May day meeting. He also added that Norman Thomas would be one of the speakers.

Crossing the street and moving in the direction of the entrance on Eighth avenue, at least a score of policemen shouted at me, "Move on." By the time I had run the gauntlet of a hundred policemen I felt like a criminal. Reaching the entrance, and having no ticket, admission was properly refused. Among the police that choked the entrance was a son of Erin (I am Irish) who had worked himself up or had been worked up into a frenzy.

He stood chattering at me and others within reach, "Move on." Glancing at him I did not know whether to laugh or be indignant.

But I moved on—with misgivings, not about the Communists, for of them I am ignorant, but about the police. For their attitude suggested that they were looking for trouble and would be disappointed if they did not find trouble. In other words, they were encouraging crime by taking a false position in relation to those peaceably assembled who were committing no crime.

Now shift the scene to Berlin, Germany, on May 1, 1930. It was a beautiful morning and shortly after breakfast I started forth to observe the Communists. Berlin, outside of Moscow, is the leading Communist center in the world. Recognizing their right to assemble, the authorities had set apart the large square at the end of Unter den Linden, flanked by the late Kaiser's palace and the massive cathedral. Arriving at the square I saw a surging mass of not less than 25,000 with red carnations, waving banners, bands of music, and singing groups. It was a weird and unforgettable sight. And the police were there even as the police were on hand in New York. But what a difference!

Yes, the police in blue uniforms that contrasted with the dominant red of the Communists were on the scene—but not unduly in evidence. They moved about firmly rather than jumpily. When a banner passed in the procession with a caricature of themselves in an ugly helmet, they even laughed. If an obstinate individual insisted upon breaking through the lines, he was good naturedly and unmistakably shown the error of his way. Their job seemed to be to protect these enthusiastic people in the exercise of their lawful right of assembly on this their great holiday. Mingling with the crowd during the hours of the day, not one policeman said to me, "Move on."

The meaning of these two experiences as thus brought into juxtaposition is apparent. As regards their theory of government these Communists are only children—at least I think so. The Bible says, "Provoke not your children to wrath." The question for the congressional commission to study is whether the police in some of our cities are violating the scriptural injunction.

A November Afternoon vs.
A May Morning

REPENTANCE seems to have fallen into ill-repute. There is plenty of fault-finding with others, and an abundance of smug satisfaction with ourselves. But of genuine soul piercing repentance there is little. This is serious and indicates moral decadence. For, when correctly understood, repentance is one of the acid tests of a strong character. Whenever you come upon an expanding personality you find a person who takes a repentant attitude in life.

Still, many are missing this thought. Repentance suggests to them an afternoon in late November with the clouds like mountains of chaos in the sky, a raw wind blowing, and withered leaves fluttering groundward. It is something austere, humiliating, to be avoided whenever possible. To use the telling phrase of another, it is "the climax of chagrin."

But this is a dreadful mistake that involves dire consequences. John the Baptist had no such thought in mind when he uttered the words, "Repent ye; for the kingdom of heaven is at hand." He was looking ahead to something better. In his mind, repentance did not mean the mere avoidance of hell, but the positive enjoyment of heaven.

Repentance, to be sure, is a courageous act, but

with the invigoration that courage always brings when directed to worthy ends. Repentance indicates joy, for the consciousness of a courageous facing of undesirable facts, and the overcoming of them, always creates a joyous feeling. Repentance means progress, for it implies dissatisfaction with present conditions and the determination to correct them. Also, repentance involves a larger freedom as the crust of respectability is broken. In short, repentance is like a beautiful May morning, with sunshine flooding the earth, foliage unfolding, and birds singing.

Moreover, those who take the repentant attitude to life are those who exert the most beneficent influence. Evidence for this is seen in many directions. For example, the parent who is genuine enough and strong enough to confess a mistake to his children does not thereby lose their respect, as some parents foolishly believe. On the contrary, his hold upon them is increased. Likewise, the teacher when a blunder has been made in discipline or teaching loses nothing in prestige by being frank with the scholars and admitting the blunder.

Some years ago the public was aroused by the conditions under which the foundations of a vast fortune had been laid. The owner of this fortune tried to overcome the opposition. He gave large sums to charity. His publicity agents pictured him as giving pennies to children as he came out of church. But he neglected the most effective method, namely, to indicate that being human he had done wrong, and had repented. A mere suggestion of repentance would have counted for more than many millions and countless pennies.

Here is a thought for the leader in industry, politics, education, and religion. Never be too respectable to repent. Remove your defense mechanisms. Be good enough to say, I want to improve. People like better the person who can sometimes say, "I was wrong," than the person who always says, "I am right." For repentance is an indication of strength, not of weakness. It means the balmy air of a beautiful May morning, not the raw wind of a somber November afternoon.

Overlooked Fact about Methuselah

IT has always seemed strange that no one, so far as I know, has ever mentioned the really important thing about Methuselah. When his name is spoken, a single thought comes into the mind. It is recalled that he holds the blue ribbon for longevity. To be exact, if free play is given to credulity, and the statement of the Bible taken literally, he lived 969 years.

That a man should live almost a thousand years is most unusual. But it has no importance because it leaves us in the dark about the man himself. It would be worth more to know how he lived one year than to know that he existed nine centuries plus sixty-nine years. Mark Twain, in a lecture dealing with Methuselah would linger for a moment upon the number of years this antique man lived. Then with the peculiar drawl that helped to make him famous would add, "What of it?" And the question went to the root of the matter. For if all that has come down about a man is the number of years he lived, then nothing of value is revealed.

But something more is recorded about Methuselah. His father's name is given. Here is a bit of information that makes less obscure this man who took such a long time to die. To have the name of a man's father is to have something to

work from in seeking to know the man himself.
For, regardless of any particular theory of heredity, to know the father is to have a slight clue
to the son.   Especially is this true if the father
is really worth knowing, as the father of Methuselah was.   Alexander the Great was the son of
Philip of Macedon, the younger Pitt was the son
of the Earl of Chatham, and Methuselah was the
son of Enoch.

Whether Methuselah was a chip of the old block
is not stated.   Let us hope he was.   For the old
block was a huge, granitic character.   If asked to
name the half dozen sublimist utterances recorded
in brief, concise form, I should not hesitate to
include the words spoken about Enoch.   Here they
are: "And Enoch walked with God: and he was
not; for God took him."   Methuselah was the
son of this man.   And this fact is worth more than
the fact that he lived 969 years.

There is, moreover, something of tremendous
importance known about Methuselah.   Curiously
enough, it has to do with the very beginning of
his life when he was a mere baby, not with the
ending of his life when he was a terribly old man.
Connected with his earliest infancy, to be sure, he
is entitled to no credit.   Nevertheless, he should
live on the page of history because of this fact.

Now, if you will read the few verses in the
Bible dealing with father and son, you will come
upon these words: "And Enoch walked with God
after he begat Methuselah."   Do you catch the
significance of the last four words—"After he

begat Methuselah"? This is, when the father looked into the face of his new-born baby boy, life took on a deeper meaning. The appearance of the helpless little infant son marked a turning point in the life of the stalwart, grown-up father. This is at once very beautiful and very human.

What the little son Methuselah did for his father Enoch, little children have been doing for their parents ever since. It is a sacred moment when a child is born into a family. Father and mother alike, if they are made of genuine stuff, will never again be the same. Like Enoch, they will begin to walk with God. And they will need thus to walk, if they are to meet their responsibility of leading the child onward into a richer and fuller life.

Taking the Soup Too Hot

T HE homely title of this article was suggested by an English writer, who, in a recent stimulating essay quotes a conversation between Dr. Johnson and his almost as famous biographer, Boswell. Having listened to the comment of his biographer upon the terrible words in the Bible regarding the doctrine of eternal punishment, Dr. Johnson remarks: "Some of the texts are indeed strong, but they admit of a mitigated interpretation." The English essayist, impressed by the relief afforded by Dr. Johnson's use of the word, "mitigated," writes, "No man takes his soup as hot as it is cooked."

This is true or ought to be true. There is no truth or experience the meaning of which is exhausted when considered from a single angle. Connected with the truth or experience is always the thought of mitigation—of never taking the soup as hot as it is cooked.

Perhaps you are troubled as many have been troubled by the language in the Bible about the justice and wrath of God. But the harshness is mitigated by other language in the Bible about the love and mercy of God.

People are disturbed in their thinking by the seeming cruelty of Nature. It appears beautiful but unfeeling. At times it presents itself as a huge platter with animal life, including man, scrambling at the edge of the platter for existence. But this picture of the survival of the fittest is mitigated by the picture of the struggle to be fit that service may be rendered. Animals will give their lives for the sake of other lives as well as take other lives for the sake of their own lives. Coöperation no less than competition prevails in Nature.

The argument for fate as applied to human life seems irresistible. If reason is given full play, every thought, impulse and action is the result of law. Each of us is a prisoner in a body's cage. Again the soup is not taken as hot as it is cooked. For the fact of law is mitigated by the fact of freedom made known to us in consciousness. The famous words, "I do not choose to run," are descriptive of life in every decision.

These words about the hot soup take on their finest meaning, however, when thought of in relation to others. Someone you know makes a stupid and costly blunder; perhaps, commits an ugly sin. Your first reaction is one of sharp and biting criticism—you want to gulp down the soup as hot as it is cooked. But are there no mitigating circumstances? Must you take the soup as hot as it is cooked? For one thing, being human, you have a marvelous capacity for making blunders and committing sins. You may have avoided making some of the blunders and of committing some of the sins. Still, the capacity is there. Then, if you knew all the facts about your friend who committed the sin or made the blunder, it is possible that you would let the soup cool a bit before taking it.

At least this is what Jesus would do as revealed by his actions and his thoughts. If I may say so with the utmost reverence, it seems to me sometimes that the mission of Jesus on earth was to cool the soup that others wanted to take too hot. Loyal to the truth of divine justice, yet eager to reveal divine love, he ever sought the mitigating circumstances. When he faced the accusers of the woman taken in adultery he said: "Let him that is without sin cast the first stone." And no stone was thrown at the poor woman. For it dawned upon their minds that their soup was too hot.

The Revolution Taking Place

IF you are tough-minded you will not be disturbed by the title of this article. Horses once shied at motor cars on the roadway. Then, as these contraptions became numerous, the horses ceased to notice them. So with the word revolution.

A few years ago men were afraid of the word. Sensing a change taking place, they used the word transition to describe the change. Later, going deeper in their interpretation of life, but still avoiding the dangerous word, revolution, they said that the change was due to the evolutionary process, whatever that might mean. But these words have been abandoned as too tame. Today, like the horse and the motor car, intelligent people walk right up to this dangerous word, and without a quiver in the voice declare that we are living in one of the three great revolutionary eras of history.

The reason for calling our age revolutionary is that changes are taking place suddenly and sometimes with shattering effect. There is nothing new in the fact of change, for it is inherent in life. But in former ages change was gradual and slow. What makes our age revolutionary is the rapidity of the change. In the Bible we read, "These that have turned the world upside down have come hither also." Forces are at work turning the world upside down.

Evidence of this is on every hand. Commerce and industry with the breath of pursuing science on their necks are uneasy. Thoughtful people are wondering whether the present business disturbance is a danger signal indicating that the limit has been reached in creating new employment to take up the slack caused by automatic machinery throwing men out of employment. If so, some far-reaching change must come.

Revolutionary tendencies are seen in other directions. A survey of the intellectual field shows the same startling change. Such recent books as "Science and Nature," by Whitehead, or John Dewey's last book, "The Quest for Certainty," challenge the very foundations of science and philosophy. These books should not, however, be read after a day of toil or following a hearty dinner.

More revolutionary still in its effect upon human welfare is the change taking place in social relations. The sinister illustration of this is family life as modified by the startling increase in the divorce rate in our own country. Havelock Ellis, an authority on the history of the family, has made the astounding statement that the divorce rate is higher in the United States than in Soviet Russia.

Cautious and ultra-conservative people are uneasy because of the menace of the "Reds." A magazine that boasts of being 100 per cent American has a department with the caption, "The Enemy at Our Gates"—the enemy being the dreadful "Reds." But this is foolish. For while we are trembling because of changes desired by political radicals, more startling changes are actually taking place. It is the part of wisdom to seek to understand the changes that are real, rather than to take counsel of our fears regarding changes that are only remotely possible.

An Unanswerable Argument

ON the railway train going to Chicago was a clean-cut young business man. In the club car he expressed to the man in the next chair, who happened to be the writer of this article, his strong disapproval of the 18th Amendment.

Having listened courteously, for the young man did most of the talking, it seemed wise to divert the conversation by inquiring as to his family. At once his face brightened and sentiment glowed softly in the eyes as he told of his wife and two little boys—ages six and nine. Soon we were good friends, for the family is the golden link in conversation that unites human hearts the world over, even though the acquaintance be casual.

When the time came to separate and seek sleep in the Pullman, I boldly suggested to the young father that upon his return home he have his two boys say their prayers at his knee. He replied that they always did when he was home. Going further, I suggested that while the little fellows were saying their prayers, he repeat to himself the objections to the 18th Amendment.

He gave me a quizzical look, as well he might. Although a business man of the high-powered salesman type, he did not know how to meet the situation. So he did what sensible men do under such conditions, he kept still. Moments of silence ensued, during which his strong face became suffused with gentleness. Then, looking me in the eye, he quietly said: "I see the point. You win." "No," I replied, "your little boys win."

And little boys should win. The broad purpose of the 18th Amendment is to make a better world into which children may be born and grow up. This being so, children are the most compelling argument in support of the Amendment.

To test this thought, think of yourself as a parent. It is bedtime hour and your child is about to do that most beautiful and sacred thing—say its prayer at your knee. While the little mannie is speaking the words of his prayer, repeat to yourself the objections that you have heard to this legislative act. Also recall the sinister fact that a few women socially prominent are forgetting their motherhood, if they are mothers, and using their influence to weaken this humane legislation. With the objections and the women in your mind, glance down at the dear little boy on his knees, and observe his trustful face looking up into your face.

If you are a genuine man, the objections about a fanatical minority having put it over, the invasion of personal liberty, the need of light wines and beer, more drinking than ever, the task, one for the states not the central government, impossibility of enforcing the law, and so on, will shrivel and drop away as leaves wither and fall groundward. If the parental instinct is tender and vibrant within you, the action of women with social pretensions so far forgetting their womanhood as to seek to destroy this noble legislation, which has as its purpose the giving to children a fairer chance to grow up, becomes utterly cruel—almost inhuman. Sounding clear and sweet above the rattle of words in objection, you will hear the beautiful words—"And a little child shall lead them."

Convictions vs. *Opinions*

IF an earnest man, you have some convictions. If a thoughtful man, you have many opinions. Your convictions are sentences in life that end with periods. Your opinions are sentences that end with interrogation points. For a conviction has in it an element of finality; an opinion a sense of uncertainty. Having a conviction indicates that you are convinced; holding an opinion implies that you would like to be convinced.

The distinction between convictions and opinions, however, goes beyond that of certainty and uncertainty. For a conviction is an opinion that has reached down and taken root in your deeper nature. An opinion is a thought that has failed to take root and become a conviction. So a conviction has depth; an opinion lies upon the surface.

Because of this, a conviction while it starts with the intellectual, ends with the moral. An opinion remains purely intellectual and concerns itself with the mental processes. Your opinion is that tomorrow may be fair and warm. Your conviction is, that regardless of the weather you must live an honorable life tomorrow. To state it even more strongly, a conviction is the voice of God in the soul of man; an opinion is the voice of the man himself whispering in his own mind.

This is the thought of the Apostle, when in one of his letters he writes, "But to the rest say I, not the Lord." Notice he seems to go out of his way to make it clear that what he has to say comes from himself, not from God. That is, he would have them know that he is expressing an opinion, not a conviction. Now this is very fine and reveals a man who has himself well in hand. For it is a mark of effective living to be able to clearly keep in mind the difference between convictions and opinions.

In actual life this is not easily done. There is ever a tendency to jumble convictions and opinions. To hold as opinions what should be possessed as convictions; and to possess as opinions what should be held as opinions, is a common enough experience. Perhaps the danger of mistaking one's opinions for convictions is more frequently met with.

Those who do this remind me of the little boy whose mother gave him pencil and paper and told him to amuse himself drawing at the dining room table. After a while she came in from the kitchen and asked him what he was drawing. He answered, "God." This shocked the mother and she said, "Why, Willie, no one in the world knows what God looks like." "Well," replied the boy, "they will when I get through." So with some of our friends who confuse their opinions and mistake them for convictions.

Most of us as we grow older become a bit suspicious of people who have an abundance of convictions. We feel that it is better to have a few convictions that reach down into the deeper nature.

On the other hand, the mere opinion attitude to life has little to attract us. For the man who is inclined to end every sentence of life with a question mark does not inspire us with confidence. To live effectively both convictions and opinions are necessary. But like the Apostle, it is necessary to know one from the other.

Laymen Who Try to Preach

A BOOK with the above title appeared a few months ago. It was a compilation, and contained sermons by a group of more or less distinguished laymen. On the jacket of the book, the names of the lay preachers were printed in two columns of six names each, with an odd name at the bottom. This made me uneasy, for here was the unlucky number 13. But my superstition was overcome by the thought that probably the compiler meant the 13 as a baker's dozen—good measure.

Reading the names, I noticed that of the 13 lay preachers, only one was a woman. A dozen men, and then to make the baker's dozen a woman thrown in for good measure—or good manners. This was a mistake. Women, no less than men, listen to preaching. Quite as many women as men pass judgment on preaching. And there are women as famous as any of the men in this book.

So, with a feeling of resentment at the unfair treatment of women; also, a desire to be gallant, I opened the book and, ignoring the men, went at once to the sermon by the solitary woman. It began as follows: "If I had only one sermon to preach perhaps I might well take as my subject the failure of modern preaching." As the sermon was read, the impression made upon my mind was that, having taken as her subject the failure of

modern preaching, this clever woman should have
given us a better example of what a really strong
sermon should be. But, having fired her opening
shot, she missed her opportunity because of
scattering her shots.

Then came the reading of the sermons by the
famous men. Here a surprise awaited me. Having been introduced to the volume by the sermon
of the woman, I expected, of course, that the men
in their sermons would criticize preaching in the
modern pulpit. Bertrand Russell, to be sure, indulged in a blanket indictment of preachers, school
teachers and judges. Dr. Joseph Collins was certain that the interpretation of religion given by
the church was wrong. But the preacher and his
sermon were left severely alone.

Why? The answer is that these men were more
concerned with giving their own messages than
with criticizing preachers and their sermons. They
were too big and had too much in their heads to
waste their time finding fault. It is the little
fellow with an empty head who lingers on the
fringe of the church and criticizes the pulpit.

The sermons which these laymen wrote, even
that of the woman, made interesting reading.
This was to be expected. Chesterton, Philip Gibbs,
Henry Seidel Canby and the others are seasoned
veterans with the pen, and could not be dull if
they tried. Still, if all the sermons made good
reading, not all of them were equally convincing.
For example, the sermon entitled "The Importance of Style." A very interesting subject, but

like some so-called sermons heard from the pulpit, this subject should be presented to a women's club, not to a church audience.

Also, one of the sermons seemed to get no-where. I read the sermon twice, and could not make heads or tails of it. This gave me positive satisfaction. For as an ordinary preacher more than once I have finished a sermon not knowing whether I was afoot or horseback. And to find a famous man preaching his very best sermon and losing his way—rather pleased me.

Nevertheless, making due allowance for the treatment of the woman, and for the brilliant man who lost his way, as I finished reading the book, the words of the Bible came into my mind, "How beautiful are the feet of them that bring glad tidings of good things," that is, preach, even just once.

Once When Words Became
Things

OF the many academic functions for the con-
ferring of honorary degrees for notable
achievement that I have witnessed, the most unique
and impressive was the recent function at the University of Vermont, when its president, Guy W.
Bailey, granted a degree to Mrs. Calvin Coolidge.

A vast audience, of whom many were former
neighbors and classmates, spontaneously rising to
pay its homage of respect and admiration to its
own. The distinguished husband, a former President of the United States, seated near-by and ad-
mirably succeeding in hiding his feelings. And
the beautiful woman herself, joyously and modest-
ly at home as she stood upon the platform—for
Burlington in a family and academic sense was her
home. Never was there a more colorful university
scene, yet aglow with sentiment like hills warmed
by sunlight in the evening hour.

But what stands out most vividly in my memory,
as this historic scene is recalled, is the presentation
by the eminent scholar, Professor Frederick
Tupper. Let me quote:

"I present for the degree of Doctor of
Laws, Grace Goodhue Coolidge, daughter of
Burlington and this University; all ours when
the school girl and college woman lived and

worked among us; ours still though not un-
shared when the First Lady cast her kindly
spell of act and speech and manner over the
heart of a nation; ours now when we honor in
her guise the crown of achievement, the art
of all arts, 'the power of grace, the magic of
a name.' "

You will never hear or read in connection with
an academic function a more perfect utterance than
this. Here in considerably less than one hundred
words, a master craftsman in the use of English
rises to the occasion and says precisely the thing
that needed to be said. Not a word too many or a
word too few. And said in simple, chaste, and
musical language as you will feel if you read these
words aloud:

"He felt the flame, the fanning wings,
 Nor offered words till they were things."

Notice also the skillful craftsmanship as seen in
the subtle play upon the word "grace," as found
near the opening and again near the close of the
utterance. "Grace Goodhue Coolidge," and "the
power of grace." This indicates the classical scholar familiar with the Greek. For in the original
language the primary meaning of this word is a
salutation. As today upon passing a friend we
say, "Good morning," so in earlier times a Greek
meeting a Greek would say, "Grace be unto you."
And this meaning has been taken over into our
religion. For grace means the loving salutation

of God as embodied in the person of Jesus. "The grace of our Lord Jesus Christ be with you."

This brings us to the final test of this utterance —its integrity. The delicate and subtle play upon the word "grace" brought out the beautiful characteristic of Mrs. Coolidge—her graciousness. For she will live in American history as a First Lady who "cast her kindly spell of act and speech and manner over the heart of the nation," as she graciously said "Good morning." And she was thus gracious because the grace of God was in her heart.

A Roof with a Ridge Pole

TRUTH seems so contradictory that some people are discouraged. They are like two men who compared their ideas about foreign cities. "London," said one, "is the foggiest place in the world." "No," objected the other, "I've been in a foggier place than London." "Where was that?" "I don't know where it was, it was so foggy." So with truth. The contradictions seem so many that they obscure and make finding difficult.

You believe in protection—but insist upon free trade in raw material. You believe in nationalism—but, unless a hopeless chauvinist, recognize the need of internationalism. You believe in capitalism as opposed to socialism—but in the name of capitalism practice socialism. You believe in individualism—but your every act is conditioned upon communism—coöperation. You believe in heredity—but perceive the effect of environment. You believe in memory—but try to forget. You believe in freedom of speech—but resent the use of indecent language in the presence of your wife. You believe in the real—but find that sometimes the ideal is the most real. You believe in faith—but insist upon works. You believe in salvation, the free gift of heaven—but live as though it came through achievement. You believe in the transcendence of Diety—but are inspired by His immanence. You kneel to worship Christ as the Son of God—but rise to follow Him as the Son of Man.

Moreover, seeming contradictions without number are found in the Bible. It is a book of paradoxes, for it is the great Book of Life. A single illustration: "Bear ye one another's burdens," it says. Yet in the same paragraph it says, "For each man shall bear his own burden." One statement seems to contradict the other statement.

This does not trouble the scientist. He meets the situation with his word, "relativity," a word made famous by Einstein. Nothing is absolute, everything is relative, even time, space and light. The philosopher comes a little nearer with his polarity of thought idea. Truth is a sphere, and over against every point of truth on the sphere is an opposite point of truth. Which is but another way of saying that every truth is a half-truth.

But this language is too technical for most of us. A simpler and clearer metaphor is that of a roof with its ridge pole. It has two sides; both sides are necessary; only one side can be seen at a time; the two sides tend to converge, the point of convergence being the ridge pole, which as regards some truths is beyond human ken.

Such a metaphor, if kept in mind, will have a practical effect upon your thinking life. It will protect you against the blatant and arrogant know-it-all attitude to truth. Modesty and humility will characterize your thinking as you avoid the danger of a false simplicity by remembering that truth, being a roof with a ridge pole, has more than one side.

Also, with this metaphor in mind, your life will breathe forth a spirit of tolerance. While loyal to the truth given, you will not forget that you are seeing but one side of the roof. Your brother man may be seeing the other side of the roof. But in heaven, let us believe, the seeming contradictions will disappear as the conceptions of truth converge at the ridge pole of reality. But in this life, "We know only in part."

Correct Form vs. *Good Manners*

AMBASSADOR DAWES lingered on the front pages of newspapers for months because of his pipe. Should he care to return to these pages with even heavier headlines, he would simply have to forget the correct fork in eating the salad at a formal dinner in London. For the American people are interested in correct form. Whether they are interested in good manners is another question. But a glance at the papers, magazines and books being published indicates a large reading public concerned with etiquette.

Correct form is not the same as good manners. In comparison, correct form is trivial. It deals with life at the surface, whereas good manners go below the surface. It has to do with outer details, and manners with inner attitude. It concerns itself with things, and manners with spirit. It is constantly changing to the delight or dismay of merchants—salad forks are a recent invention. Manners remain relatively fixed.

There is no necessary connection between correct form and good manners. You may have the form and lack the manners; you may have the manners and lack the form. A man unaccustomed to social amenities makes many blunders and still remains a gentleman. Another man at home in the most sophisticated social circles is only a cad.

But correct form and good manners are not contradictory. There is no inevitable connection between them; and one is of much more importance than the other. Nevertheless, a wise man will act on the theory, "This ought ye to have done, and not to have left the other undone." For it is a principle of life that little things determine big issues. The back of the camel is broken by the straw; the evenly balanced scale is swerved by the feather; and the massive train is derailed by the stone. It is with this principle in mind that the Bible says, "Despise not the day of small things" —even dress, eating and other things.

Being a genius, of course you can despise the small things. Mark Twain appeared in an evening dress suit of white. Whistler refused to wear a tie, insisting that a tie was inartistic and marred the effect of a white shirt front. Napoleon when dining, if he did not like a certain dish being served, brushed it from the table to the floor. You can do such whimsical and crude things if you are a genius. But be sure of your credentials.

A man missed becoming the president of one of our greatest universities, because he mistakenly thought himself a genius. The story is this: The governing board of this university surveyed the field of candidates and found the choice had narrowed down to two men. Both men possessed marked ability and sterling characters. So it was six of one and half a dozen of the other. But in meeting the men socially the officials noticed that one man was careless in using his knife at the table. The other man had correct form as regards using his fork. To mix the metaphors, the knife of one man was the straw that broke his camel's back; the fork of the other man was the feather that caused the scale to dip in his favor.

Correct form does not make a gentleman. But the value of a gentleman's life will be much enhanced by the observance of correct form—if not overdone.

Good Manners vs. *Correct Form*

I F the reader honored me by reading the preceding essay, he has observed that the subject then differed from the subject of this essay only in a transposition of the words. Then, correct form preceded good manners, because it was shown that although inferior to good manners, correct form has value. In this essay good manners precede correct form, because it will be pointed out how manners suffer when form is carried too far.

A historic instance of form being overdone is Lord Derby, prime minister of England, standing before Queen Victoria. The statesman, no longer young and in ill health, had been summoned to Windsor. Regardless of his health he obeyed. When ushered into her presence, the Queen, observing that he was very ill, remarked: "I am sorry that etiquette does not allow me to ask you to be seated."

The Queen was right in saying that etiquette did not allow her to ask him to be seated. That is, etiquette was so strong that good manners did not have a chance. Here is an example of correct form having changed into rigid form and making impossible something finer than form. It would be going too far to say that the Queen displayed bad manners. She simply failed to express good manners.

But insistence upon form sometimes leads to bad

manners. A striking illustration is in connection with another prime minister—the recent visit of Ramsey MacDonald and his daughter to this country.

A petty feud had existed between the sister of the Vice-President and the wife of the Speaker of the House regarding social precedence. At first it was amusing, then tiresome, and at the time of the visit of the distinguished statesman and his daughter, disgusting. Because of these two women, social functions were disarranged, and even the invitation of President Hoover was declined by one woman because the other woman had been given precedence.

About the merits of this squabble I know little and care less. It is mentioned to show how emphasis upon mere form leads to action that is unkind. For good manners is a kindly attitude—a desire to have others feel at ease. This involves thinking less of self than of other selves. Christ has been called the first gentleman of the world. Although the words are inadequate, they do express the spirit of Christ's life—His eagerness to have others feel His friendly relation. And it was while at a dinner more famous than any ever held in Washington that He defined good manners when He said: "I am in the midst of you as one that serveth."

By insisting upon their rights, Dollie Gann and Alice Longworth missed their opportunity for gracious service. As mere sticklers for correct form they displayed bad manners. And the charming

English girl, Ishbel MacDonald—the official guest of the nation—captured the blue ribbon for good breeding. For when asked where she would like to sit at one of the formal dinners, she replied: "Near somebody nice to talk to." This is what they call in England the sporting spirit, which at its finest is simply good manners.

The Story of a Real Estate Deal

IF you want to read a perfect gem of a short story, turn to the account of Abraham buying a burial lot. For suavity of approach and seeming willingness to yield much only to gain more, the characters in this story make the average real estate agent look like a mere peddler of shoe strings.

The story is this: Sarah, the wife of Abraham, has died. Like most people he has made no provision for this inevitable event. But with her body awaiting burial he must act. So he selects a particular cave in the corner of a field. The owner is approached and found willing to sell this land. A price is agreed upon and the deal is about to be closed.

Then something happens that gives the story its peculiar flavor and meaning. In describing the property in the deed, as we would say today, more is described than was mentioned during the negotiations. For Abraham has added these words: "And all the trees that were in the field, that were in all the border thereof round about."

The question is, Why does Abraham, having successfully concluded the negotiations for the burial lot, insist upon a mention of the trees? According to our custom, unless expressly stipulated otherwise, the trees would go with the land. But Abraham not only has them mentioned, but he

121

adds the word "all."   Not a single tree must be omitted.

It is possible, of course, that the trees are an illustration of the baker's dozen—just thrown in for good measure.   Perhaps there is here an example of this wealthy old man's business sagacity. Trees had commercial value.   Or here is evidence of Abraham's love of the beautiful.   There is nothing more beautiful than trees.   Still these explanations do not quite meet the situation.

His heart rather than his head is speaking in these words about the trees.   For they are the oaks of Mamre.   Under these trees he and his wife had lived for many years.   More than once as he returned from a journey he had seen his wife seated in the shade of one of these oaks.   So now, he asks that all the trees may be preserved on the burial lot.   He will lay the body of Sarah gently in the ground and then think of the wind sighing in the trees and the shadows from the branches being thrown athwart her last resting place.

It is only a little touch, these words about the trees, but a touch that reveals Abraham as a man of sentiment.   Yet these little touches are oftentimes the shafts of light that shoot down into the depths and reveal a man.   When John Marshall passed away they found a wisp of the hair of his wife in a locket next to his body.   Abraham Lincoln is seen leaving his carriage and tenderly lifting a little bird with a broken wing back to its nest. Edmund Burke, having lost his only boy, went at the close of the day to the pasture that he might pat the neck of the horse that his boy rode. And Abraham, his heart touched by sentiment, asked that every tree on the lot be included in the trans-action—for his beloved Sarah loved trees.

"Oh, the little more and how much it is!
And the little less, and what worlds away!"

Religion with a Rocking Chair

"THE Rocking-Chair Church" is the name of a place of worship in a small town in the South. The story of the name is this: A small boy attended divine worship. Coming out of church, he said to his parents that if there were rocking-chairs instead of pews, he would attend every Sunday. The little fellow was in delicate health and lived but a few years. After his death, his father, remembering his unusual remark, had the pews removed and rocking-chairs installed in the church.

Something of this kind has been done with religion in recent years. Seeking to make religion more attractive, the comfortable rocking-chair of easy thinking and acting has replaced the rather uncomfortable straight-backed pew of vigorous thought and deed. In many pulpits the robust doctrinal sermon has given way to the thin, snappy, so-called practical talk. Zealous workers, seeking for a record in church membership, have button-holed people to sign up. Evidence of a change of heart as a condition of church membership is considered old-fashioned and out of date.

What has been the result? Having visited more than fifty churches in different parts of the country in recent months, perhaps I am qualified to express an opinion. The evidence is unmistakable that stupendous sums of money have been invested in church buildings. Also, the evidence is clear that large numbers have been added to the rolls of the churches. But, turning from the beautiful buildings and the statistics of membership to actual attendance at the services of divine worship, the situation is less hopeful. To state it more definitely, the impression made upon my mind is that the churches are losing their hold upon the young people in their late teens and early twenties. If you doubt this, glance over the congregation next Sunday morning and count the number of such young people present.

This easy-going, genial, flabby, rocking-chair kind of religion does not interest young people. And there are reasons for this. One is that the rocking-chair idea is essentially false. Young people are concerned with life, and life has something austere and grim. Gray clouds and cold winds, no less than sunshine and balmy air, abound in life. To present religion as merely a burst of sunlight is to contradict reality as young people experience life.

Another reason is that religion conceived of as a rocking-chair presents a false simplicity. On its human side religion deals with character. But character means struggle—something to be won, not merely acquired. Young people demand stiffening of the spine, not encouragement in taking a nap. In other words, they require straight-backed pews, not rocking-chairs.

There is another reason, and the most important, because often overlooked. That which is difficult is more attractive to virile, healthy people than that

which is easy.   The very elements that some ministers avoid in order to be popular are the elements
that attract young people who are facing life
earnestly.   They will select the straight-backed
chairs in a room, leaving the rocking-chair for
grandmother.

This austere, grim, battling kind of religion is
the only kind found in the Bible.   It knows nothing of the glad hand, good mixer, chicken pie
supper kind of religion.   The older Paul writing to
the younger Timothy said, "Suffer hardship with
me, as a good soldier of Christ Jesus."   He
understood young people.

What about Travel and Education?

TO what extent is education secured through travel? The question is interesting because of the number of people who are being lured into travel, thinking that thereby they will gain in education.

That travel is related to education admits of no doubt. Darwin made his epochal interpretation of evolution because of material gathered during the long voyage of the *Beagle*. Professional men travel to increase their skill. Artists go to Paris; economists, theologians and musicians go to Berlin; and physicians and surgeons go to Vienna. Moreover, individuals, granted they have inner resources, react educationally to the changing wonders of nature and human nature as they journey in distant parts.

Still the question has to do with the average person who gallivants over the earth, dodging in and out of art galleries and cathedrals in Europe, or tarries long enough to feed the bears, as he hurries through Yellowstone Park. The question is, Does this person receive any education as the result of his travel? In giving an answer, let me present three considerations which will tend to check any undue enthusiasm about the educational aspect.

One is, if there is educational value in travel,

then the American people are the most educated people in the world. Where those of other nations travel one mile, Americans are journeying ten miles by train, steamship, motor car and aeroplane. If the measure of an individual's education is the extent to which he has traveled, then Pericles, Socrates, Thucydides and the others of the Golden Age of Greece were mere ignoramuses in comparison with the average American today. Yet none of us would care to make such an absurd statement. Distance traversed is no indication of education.

Again, compare a group of widely traveled persons with a group of thoughtful persons who have traveled little. At a luncheon in Berlin a dozen men gathered. We were from five continents. The conversation fairly bubbled with all kinds of interesting information. Yet the group did not impress me as more thoughtful than a like number of business and professional men, with slight travel experience, that might gather about a table in any live American community. No, information is not education.

Further, draw upon your knowledge of history and recall that with few exceptions the great thinkers of the race have never wandered far. Shakespeare beat a path not many miles long from Stratford to London. The inventor of the internal combustion engine—the most fundamental invention of the modern world—spent his life in a German village. Christ, the spiritual genius of the race, moved in an area less than half the size of Massachusetts.

Travel if you must on errands of mercy or business. Travel if you will for health or pleasure. But before starting forth read Emerson's famous essay on "Self-Reliance." It will make some of the circulars of tourist agencies dealing with the educational value of travel seem pretty flimsy. In fact, if you have traveled far and are not compelled to travel this summer, it might be well to remain at home and do a little thinking. For there is an old jingle as follows:

"A young American crossed the ocean by chance,
  Learned his morals in London, his manners in
      France,
  A student in Germany, an artist in Rome,
  A superlative jackass when he got home."

A Few Drops Added to the Torrent

A FLOOD of advice is coming down upon young people who this month are graduating from high school and college. Let me add my tiny rivulet.

Your first question has to do with getting a job. Prosaic as it sounds, you have to deal with the problem of food, clothing and shelter.

Along with this question of sheer existence is another question that you will do well to consider at once. In the Bible, according to a modern translation, is the injunction, "Keep in harmony with one another." That is, practice the art of living with others. This is the second most important question in life. That you must live with others is an indubitable fact. At your elbow in store, factory, office and school will be others. The question is whether you can develop such skill that your living with others becomes an art.

In considering this question beware of two false assumptions. One is that, having a keen mind, you will live a successful life. This is not necessarily true. There are almost as many clever men as stupid men failing today. The other is, if you live a clean life the problem of getting along with others will take care of itself. Not by any means. Good people are sometimes difficult to live with. Political enemies of Gladstone asked a conundrum:

Why is he like a lobster? And the answer was, Because he is so good, but agrees with no one.

Essential as character and intelligence are, something more is needed. Living with others is an art and must be learned, although like other arts some possess a special aptitude. As you go forth to acquire the art let me make four suggestions:

First, never forget that you will always have to live with yourself. When the day's work is done you may withdraw from the company of others. But only during sleep can you get away from yourself. Because of this, at whatever cost maintain your own self-respect. For no person is able to live harmoniously with others who is unable to live decently with himself.

Again, through appreciation and sympathy acquire a genuine respect for those you constantly come in contact with. Each life is an original package. Therefore each life in temperament, viewpoint, native ability or experience will be unlike yourself. One test of your skill in practicing the art of living with others will be your ability to live successfully with persons who are different. The acid test, however, of your skill will be in living harmoniously with those whom you positively dislike. And you will have to live with people who are either different or disagreeable.

A third thought is, observe carefully and if possible know those who to an unusual degree command the respect of their fellow men in the community in which they live. In every instance you will discover that the secret of their influence is found in the fact that they practice skillfully the art of living with others. There is a man in your city who on his way to business each morning makes the newsboy feel like an emperor as he greets him. This man has a genius for friendship.

The final suggestion is, connect yourself with some worth-while organization outside your work. In plying your trade, conducting your business or practicing your profession you will be compelled to live with others. Seek a fellowship where voluntarily you can perfect your skill in the art. And such a fellowship is the church. For notwithstanding its limitations, in the church as nowhere else in this imperfect world the art of living together is being practiced.

The Cloven Foot and the Angel's Wing

IF one of our interesting biographers—Lytton Strachey, Emil Ludwig, Gamalial Bradford, Stephen Benet, Bernard Fay or André Maurois— should read this article will he accept it as a challenge to try his skill on Jacob, that bewildering and fascinating character, the material for whose portraiture is found on the pages of Genesis.

The older biographers could not accept such a challenge. Because, until recently, biography has been considered a branch of history. It was the attempt to interpret a period of history by a study of some character that played a dominant part in shaping the events that made the period. Carlyle had this in mind when he said that history is biography. Neitzsche stated it more strongly when he said that a nation was a detour taken by God that He might produce more great men.

Today it is otherwise. Biographies are more fictional than historical. This does not mean that they are unreal. For great fiction as written by a Victor Hugo, George Eliot or Nathaniel Hawthorne is profoundly real. But it does mean that the biographer pays little attention to sound historical method. He does not bother with footnotes and his opinions are given without furnishing the reader with references to source material upon which his opinions are based.

133

The biographer of yesterday drew an ample background and in the foreground placed his character. The biographer of today pays slight heed to the setting, but focalizes his attention upon the personality of his character. He reads every scrap of material in the form of letters and documents having to do with the individual. With these things before him, under the guidance of psychoanalysis as taught by Jung and Freud, he seeks to trace the interaction of the conscious and unconscious in the life of the great man he is studying. Then, having soaked his mind in the material, he comes up dripping and proceeds to place upon the printed page his impressions in the form of a word portraiture.

And being more fictional than historical it makes mighty interesting reading. Some of it is great fiction and so is profoundly true. For example, Lytton Strachey's "Victoria," and André Maurois' "Disraeli."

Now supposing one of these gifted psycho-analytical biographers tries his skill upon that strange Old Testament character called Jacob. The world is waiting for the biographer with psychological insight deep enough to understand this Hebrew who moved across vast stretches and cast a long shadow. If he can really master the meaning of the personality of this antique man, he will produce one of the great biographies of history.

In writing this portraiture the biographer's problem will be this: Was Jacob a man who primarily sought to do the will of God, and incidentally to achieve success? Or was he a man whose over-mastering desire was success, and who tried to use God to realize his desire?

Du Maurier was for many years a cartoonist. When he became famous as the author of "Trilby," there was a demand for a likeness of him. So, there appeared in the London *Punch* a picture of himself and drawn by the cartoonist. But to his human form the artist added the wings of an angel and the cloven feet of the devil. Thus was Jacob. There is the angelic wing; also the cloven foot. Which is dominant?

While we are waiting for the biographer to tell us, it might be well to read the story in Genesis. For it is more interesting than any modern biography.

Have You Any Limitations?

IT is assumed that ordinary persons have limitations. What causes surprise is to come upon extraordinary persons who confess their limitations. Being exceptional, it is taken for granted that they can do anything that needs to be done.

One reason for this belief in the limitless possibilities of great men is that their lives show an ability to accomplish the seemingly impossible. Obstacles that others believe insurmountable are by them surmounted. They do with the last letter in the pesky little word "can't" what the patriots of Boston in the Revolutionary days did with the tea. Possessing indomitable wills, what they do rather than what they leave undone attracts our attention.

Another reason for missing the limitations in great men is that their lives sometimes reveal a marvelous versatility. Benjamin Franklin carried on a correspondence in five languages, experimented with stoves, lightning rods and countless other devices—apparently able to do anything. Leonardo blended the technique and dreams of the master artist with the restless inquisitiveness of the pioneer scientist—equally at home in both fields. The versatility of these men is so marked that it hides their limitations.

Yet a careful reading of biography will show that extraordinary men no less than ordinary men have their limitations. In fact, it can be shown from the page of biography that men became great because of their willingness to recognize their limitations. Also that men met with disaster through their refusal to admit that there was anything they could not do. Let the shoemaker stick to his last, is a maxim constantly encountered in history. The ability to achieve mightily within clearly defined limitations, it seems to me, is the most valuable lesson learned from the reading of the life stories of famous men.

A striking illustration of this is in the Bible narrative dealing with Moses. By common consent he belongs among the half-dozen compelling characters of history. To him was given the stupendous task of establishing a new nation by leading a people out of bondage into freedom and formulating for the people their fundamental law.

When the leadership in this gigantic undertaking was thrust upon him, with becoming modesty and clear insight he shrank from accepting. For he knew that involved in this work would be the gift of speech. This he lacked. So he replied: "But, Lord, I am no speaker—I am slow of speech, I have no command of words." He was a man of masterful action, not a prophet of fluent speech. And he was great enough to see his defect. Because of this, another was given the important work of public utterance, while he devoted himself to the mighty task of constructive statesmanship.

If great men like Moses recognize their limitations, certainly it is the part of wisdom for ordinary men like ourselves to do the same. Many of us are merely puttering with life through attempting tasks that we are not fitted to perform. It is an indication of strength, not weakness, to admit a limitation.

How Much Is the Common Man Worth?

THE worth of the common man has always been recognized. Go back as far as you can in history and evidence of man's worth will be found. Kings were able to rule only as ordinary men with bows and arrows, spears or firearms defended them. They were able to live sumptuously in palaces only as human beings toiled in fields, forests or quarries. When they died royal tombs in the form of pyramids received their bodies because of the labor of untold thousands. There has never been any doubt about the worth of the common man.

From whence is his worth derived? This is the real question that men have asked, and never more than today. The answers to this question are four in number. First, the worth of man is derived from the king who rules over him. This is the old doctrine of the divine right of kings—a doctrine that has disappeared from the modern world.

Another answer is that the worth of the individual is derived from the state. This idea came into history by way of England. The classic illustration is the Somerset case as decided by Lord Mansfield. A slave had been brought by his owners from Virginia to England, and the question was whether upon reaching England he ceased to be a slave. In this celebrated decision the judge decided that when his feet touched the soil of England the slave became a free man.

Still a third answer that marks a further advance in the doctrine is that found in the Virginia Bill of Rights which declares that man derives his worth from Nature. Man is born with certain inalienable rights. This conception is basic in the Declaration of Independence and is carried over into the Declaration of the Rights of Man in the French Revolution, almost literally in the words of George Mason.

But there is a fourth answer to this question. To find this answer it is necessary to sweep back through the centuries to the teaching of Jesus in the Bible. As you do so, you come upon the noble conception that the worth of man is derived from God. The expression of this truth is found in the single word "Father" as used by Jesus. Again and again the thought flashes from the page of the New Testament that mankind is one great family and that God is the Father of the family. Being a child of God every human being has untold worth, and not merely worth enough to bear firearms, build palaces and rear pyramids. Because of his divine origin the humblest man must never be counted out, and is entitled to respect on the basis of what he is, not because of what he has. This is spiritual democracy.

This thought of spiritual democracy needs to be pondered as we approach the Fourth of July. In our own land and in other lands there is much that contradicts this lofty idea. The difficulties encountered in attempting to create a finer society under law seem almost insurmountable. That men should be found eager to resist the tendency to organize the nations of the earth on a basis of peace is difficult to understand. Or that men should be willing to give of their time and effort to weaken a law that aims at the banishment of strong drink from our land is most discouraging.

Yet, if we learn the patience of history and take the long view, it is seen that progress has been made. Moreover, this progress has been resisted at every step. The men who have stood for a better world have been cannonaded in one generation, only to be canonized in the next generation. So let us renew our courage, take another hole in our belts, and practice more effectively the doctrine of spiritual democracy.

Two Kinds of Inspiration

IT is a familiar fact that men are inspired to do exceptional things in a given direction by other men who have done similar things in the same direction. Goethe, after spending the morning in the garden with Herder, departed with the resolve to devote his life to literature. Jewett, the noble teacher of chemistry at Oberlin College, nourished a thought in the mind of his pupil Hall, the result being the discovery of the process of commercially extracting aluminum from boxite, and which led to the founding of the aluminum industry in America. Many a preacher, artist, musician, merchant, or inventor traces the beginning of his successful career to another having followed the same career.

There is another kind of inspiration, less often considered, but none the less important. It is that of a person who, by doing a certain kind of work, inspires another person to do a different kind of work. To this kind of inspiration the Bible has reference when it says of Moses, "He shall serve as a mouthpiece for you, and you shall inspire him." Moses could not speak in public, for he had no oratorical gift. But he could so live his life as a statesman as to inspire Aaron to be an orator. The thing that he lacked, through the inspiration of his life, would be supplied in another life.

What Moses did in relation to Aaron is being done in life today. Here is a manufacturing con-

cern. Its manager has no technical skill as regards
the manufacture of the goods. He is a financial
and commercial expert rather than an industrial
expert. But he can so meet the responsibilities of
his own position as to inspire every member of
his vast organization. There are thousands of men
giving the best that is in them, because of the inspiration of the manager whose particular work is
unlike their own.

In the community is a man who is having an
honorable and successful career in business. Each
morning he leaves his home, and each evening he
returns. The active hours of the day are spent
in business; the quiet hours of the evening are
spent in the home. As you learn the secret of
his poise and strength you discover that it is due
in no small measure to the wife who makes the
home. Like Moses, unable to be an orator, this
woman is unable to transact the business, but also
like Moses she can furnish the inspiration.

There is a family of four—father, mother, son
and daughter. The father and mother are now
aged. The daughter is now in middle life. The
earnings of the father have always been modest
For years the mother has been an invalid. When
the children were younger the question of college
arose. Both were talented. But the daughter
was needed in the home because of the health of the
mother. So the son went to college and later to the
medical school. Today he is one of the leading
surgeons of America. Yet he knows and gladly admits it, that the thought of his talented sister mak-

ing the sacrifice and remaining at home has been the inspiration in his own life. She could not become a surgeon, but she could live in such a way as to inspire her brother to be a great surgeon.

Ghosts, Books, and Fools

LITERARY skill has often been employed by others without its identity being revealed. Washington's Farewell Address was whipped into shape by Alexander Hamilton, although his name nowhere appears in the manuscript. Secretaries frequently prepare talks which business men later at banquets give haltingly and with the embarrassment of school boys. Prolific writers, such as H. G. Wells and Dumas, whose output is obviously in excess of their capacity, use collaborators. Of the elder Dumas the story is told, that meeting his younger son, Alexandre, he inquired, "Have you read my latest novel?" "No," was the disconcerting reply, "have you?"

But a new situation has developed in the literary world as revealed in a gossipy book about books recently published, and written by the proprietor of a bookstore well known in New England.

This author devotes a few pages to the subject of "ghosts." In the book trade, so he tells us, those who write books which are published under other names are called "ghosts." This, he informs us, has become a recognized and lucrative business. He states that he has a friend who makes $25,000 a year as a "ghost" writer of books. This friend has published several books under his own name, but never with success. Only when his writing has been published under other names has he been successful. In fact, he has been so successful that in one year he produced a "best seller" for the man who paid him.

Here is an astounding statement. But it is made by the proprietor of a reputable bookstore. What disturbs us, however, is that he makes the statement as unconcernedly as he would flick a fly from his coat sleeve. There is no intimation that he is ashamed of the situation. On the contrary he assures us that the practice of "ghost writing" is recognized and lucrative. Further, if you please, his friend by playing the role of "ghost" makes each year a sum in five figures.

What it means is this: A man with ability prepares a manuscript. This he sells to another man who has more money and ambition than literary skill. Then the publisher skillfully advertises the book which is the property of the man who has bought something he lacks the brains to produce. Over against this situation place the deathless letter of the Apostle Paul which closes with these words: "See with how large letters I have written unto you with my own hand." As the modern book written by the "ghost" is compared with the letter written by the man who signed his own name, the contrast is presented between light and dark, between truth and falsehood.

Notice that these words about the literary "ghost" were not written by a zealous member of the Watch and Ward Society, but by a bookseller who writes approvingly of what he describes. And this incidental glimpse into the book trade indicates the depths to which the publishing business has sunk. Also, the glimpse afforded suggests that if some cities rank low as regards the number of books its citizens are buying, this may be due to the fact that at the present time there are more sensible people in these cities than in some other cities. For a person feels foolish when he has been deceived into buying a "ghost" when he thought he was buying a real book.

Skillful Nose Counting

IT was said of Mary Anne, the quaint wife of Disraeli, that she could never remember which came first, the Greeks or the Romans. Those of us with unchronological minds, and no flair for statistics, can sympathize with Mary Anne. For a statistical barrage to disturb our comfort daily is being laid in the form of population figures of states, counties, cities, and villages.

This nose-counting business, called taking the census, is not a modern contrivance. Man has always been a counting animal. In the dim past he counted his fingers and toes. This led to the invention of the numeral system—one of the great inventions of the race. Then counting on a large scale began. And for centuries the many have been counted by the few.

As far as history informs me, the earliest record of counting on a large scale is in the Bible. The opening chapter of the Book of Numbers—an appropriately dreary and colorless title for a book dealing with statistics, has the story of the first census taken of the Jews. Moses and Aaron were the director generals. Twelve men whose names are given were the divisional directors. On a certain day at designated places the clans assembled for registration by families and the numbering of the males physically able to bear arms.

But if the counting of noses is not a modern

contrivance, the thoroughness with which it is done is distinctly modern. All that was sought in earlier days was the population of the clans as based upon the families, and the number of men over twenty years of age able to bear arms in defense of the clan. Today the enumerator, to hold to the figure of speech, not only counts noses but the very wrinkles on the faces. He succeeds in doing this, notwithstanding the effort of the gentler sex to cover over the wrinkles. For, taking his life in his hand, he asks point blank the age of each one counted. In olden times women were not considered of enough worth to be counted. Today women are the point of attack in making the count.

Moreover, the statistical method by which greater accuracy is attained belongs to our day. Figures play such an important part in life that it is difficult to realize that the science of statistics, due to the work of Quetelet, the Belgium economist, dates back less than a hundred years.

In the ancient world figures were handled loosely. For instance, Joseph the Prime Minister of Egypt stored grain in anticipation of a famine. The narrative says, "He accumulated grain in huge quantities, like the sand of the sea." A modern statistician would state the exact number of bushels in the grain elevators. In dealing with Scipio's expedition to Africa and wishing to stress the bigness of his army, the historian says "that birds fell from heaven at the noise of shouting soldiers." Today, the nations that engaged in the World War can give the exact number of men that enlisted in their armies and navies.   So with census statistics. In the Book of Numbers the population of clans is given in even hundreds.   Evidently they did some guessing.   The census of 1930 announces the population of Chicago as 3,373,753.   Less guessing and more accuracy.

Any day now the last fact will be tossed upon the vast and variable pile of statistical facts made by the census.   Then the question will arise, What to do with the enormous mass?   For the meaning of life is never found in the accumulation of facts, but in the interpretation of the facts accumulated.   But of this something in the next article.

My Old Soldier's Home-Made Sign

AFTER the lapse of many years I can still see the old soldier seated under his sign. He was a veteran of the Civil War, and had lost a leg and received four wounds at the battle of Gettysburg. Having a family of five children to support, and being handicapped as a bread winner, he appeared each year at the County Fair with some shoe strings and lead pencils for sale. To attract customers he had a sign made which read as follows:

"An Old Soldier; One Leg, Four Wounds,
Five Children—Total Ten."

Here was a character as quaint in his way as Mary Anne of the last article, and like her was utterly helpless in the presence of statistics. Yet statistics have possibilities, even though they have marked limitations. To use them efficiently skill is required. For there is a science of statistics. Further, to use them helpfully integrity is demanded. The well-worn saying that figures will lie because liars will figure, finds confirmation daily.

Granted skill and integrity, figures are of untold value when applied to things that can be weighed, measured, and handled. A business man seeks a loan. The banker asks for a statement. If accurately made the statement serves as a guide in negotiating the loan.

When applied to human beings statistics have less value. The reason for this is that every person is a thing plus ideas and ideals which are radically different from things. The census being taken deals with persons as things. It tells us how many human things there are in the United States. A geographical center of population for these human things is located somewhere in the Mississippi Valley. How many of these human things live in communities of 2500 and less, and how many in communities over this number is stated. These and many other facts will be told.

But there are more vital questions that need to be answered. For instance, are the people as a whole more intelligent in 1930 than in 1920? Again, are the moral standards of the people improving? These are basic questions. For as the population increases and the shift to urban life continues, the strain upon our democratic institutions grows greater. This strain can be met only by an improvement in the intelligence and the morality of the people. Alas, this tremendous census may not answer these questions.

Yet, the distinction between the possibilities of statistics as applied to things and the limitations of statistics when confronted by ideas and ideals, need not be drawn too sharply. For life seen at the level of things sometimes suggests life at the higher level of ideas and ideals. To illustrate: In the Bible is the beautiful story of the multitude being fed. The story as told includes a few statistics. 1—the Christ; 5000—the crowd; 5 and 2—the loaves and fish; and 12—the filled baskets of food left over. These figures at least indicate an interest on the part of a crowd in the teaching of Christ, and the mysterious, sympathetic, and generous power of Christ in being able to appease the hunger of this crowd by multiplying the few loaves and fishes.

So with the census of 1930. If it shows a relative increase in the number seeking an education, and a like increase in the number assembling for worship in the churches, then the inference will be justified that America is growing in morality and intelligence.

The Second Most Important Man

W HO is this man? He is not the exceptional man at the head of the line or the ordinary man well down the line, but the efficient man that stands well up the line. Tomorrow, if conditions change, he may be at the head. Or, if he lack the last bit of tough fiber that makes the outstanding leader, he may continue next the head. Today, however, as the second most important man he is playing a vital part in business, political, and educational life.

But he is in the background. When the directors of the business gather around the table to receive the reports, he is missing. Because of this he rarely gets a square deal. At least this is true as regards public recognition. When some signally successful enterprise is featured in the newspapers, the one and the many are mentioned—the one who leads and the many who follow. But this man in between the one and the many is overlooked.

Yet, if the second most important man is largely ignored, save as he comes in under a blanket commendation of the personnel of the organization in the annual report of the president, he is not forgotten in the Bible. For the Book has a way of never passing by anything of worth. In this respect it goes deeper into life and is more up to date than the last book from the press.

To make this clear, think of an experience in the life of Moses, that mighty leader of the antique world. He was at the head of an enterprise greater than any manufacturing, commercial, political, or educational enterprise of our day. His task was to transform a mob numbering millions into an ordered nation, and establish this nation in its permanent place of abode. But like many a business man in our modern world he found his task growing too big for him. Being a big man himself, he perceived the need of gathering about him a group of men to assist in carrying on the business. As the narrative states, men who "shall share the burden of the people with you, instead of you bearing it by yourself." Here you have the second most important men—men who shall share in carrying the load.

What shall be the qualifications of these men? In language picturesque and beautiful, the Eternal is revealed as speaking and directing Moses to select seventy of the sheiks of Israel whom he knew to be men of authority in their respective circles. That is, to translate these words into the language of our day, these men were not to be ordinary men whether of the strong muscle or the white collar type, but men of marked ability. Moreover, their ability must be authoritative. Some men have a maximum of knowledge with a minimum of action. These men are to do things. For they are to be the second most important men in a stupendous enterprise, and share with Moses the task of leadership. Or, as we should say today, they were to be the executives in a great organization.

Something more is required. Having directed Moses to increase his organization by the selection of able men, the Eternal is pictured as saying to Moses, "And I will endue them with a part of your spirit." This is significant. Units, for example, in business, as they grow bigger tend to develop a weakness. This weakness is located, not in the unrest of the rank and file down the line but in the disloyal ambitions of the few near the head of the line. A man with ability above the average, unless he have more than ability, is sometimes a troublesome proposition. The second most important man at his best is one who understands the methods and aims of his leader, and is so loyal to those methods and aims that the leader can trust him.

Such able and trustworthy men exist in large numbers, although not often recognized. To them I offer this tribute, hoping that it may be read by the more prominent leaders whom these second most important men so faithfully serve.